i will plant you a lilac tree

i will plant you a lilac tree

a memoir of a Schindler's list survivor

LAURA HILLMAN

 HAMPTON-BROWN

From I WILL PLANT YOU A LILAC TREE by Laura Hillman. Copyright © 2005 by Laura Hillman.
Reprinted with permission of Atheneum Books for Young Readers,
Simon & Schuster Children's Publishing Division. All rights reserved.

Front and back cover photograph "Perimeter fence at Buchenwald" © by Ira Nowinski/CORBIS.

Cover photograph of the author as a young woman courtesy of Laura Hillman.

Map on pp. 10-11 by Rick Britton.

The reproduced portions of Schindler's List on p. 152 are courtesy of the Yad Vashem Archive.
Photographs on p. 24, 42, 182, and 202 are courtesy of Laura Hillman.

On-Page Coach™ (introductions, questions, on-page glossaries),
The Exchange, back cover summary © Hampton-Brown.

Hampton-Brown
P.O. Box 223220
Carmel, California 93922
800-333-3510
www.hampton-brown.com

Printed in the United States of America

ISBN-13: 978-0-7362-3192-3
ISBN-10: 0-7362-3192-7

06 07 08 09 10 11 12 13 14 15 10 9 8 7 6 5 4 3 2 1

In loving memory of my parents,
Martin and Karoline Wolff,
and my brothers, Wolfgang and Selly,
who were murdered by the Nazis.
May their memory live on forever.

To my husband, Bernhard Hillman, of blessed memory

Acknowledgments

I would like to thank Professor Elliot Fried of Long Beach State University for going far beyond what was expected when teaching me the craft of writing.

To my young friend Megan Stidham and her mother, Kelly Stidham, who were the sparks that led to publication of this my book, I am forever indebted to them.

To my grandsons, Aryeh and Joshua, who cheered me on to keep writing.

To the many friends who read parts of the manuscript, advised me, reassured me, and didn't let me give up.

To my friend, Larry Mendelson, who went out of his way to help.

To my editor, Robert O. Warren, for his consistent support, good sense, and good taste.

My heartfelt thanks goes out to all of you.

Introduction

It took Laura Hillman years to face the terrible circumstances and **degradation** she experienced as a prisoner in the concentration camps during World War II. Eventually she realized that her story needed to be told so she wrote this **autobiography**, *I Will Plant You a Lilac Tree*.

Hillman was born Hannalore Wolff in 1923 in Aurich, Germany. She was the eldest of five children in a middle-class Jewish family. Hannalore's life changed after Adolf Hitler, Germany's ruthless dictator, came to power. Her father was forced into a concentration camp and was killed six weeks later. Soon after, the rest of the family was sent to concentration camps where Jewish people and other people hated by Hitler experienced daily **violations** of human rights, such as torture, starvation, imprisonment, and death. Hannelore was nineteen years old. Before the horror ended, Hannelore lived in eight different concentration camps.

Hitler began World War II by invading Poland in 1939.

Key Concepts

degradation *n.* being treated with hatred or disrespect

autobiography *n.* story of a person's life that is written by that person

violation *n.* failure to respect a law, right, or rule

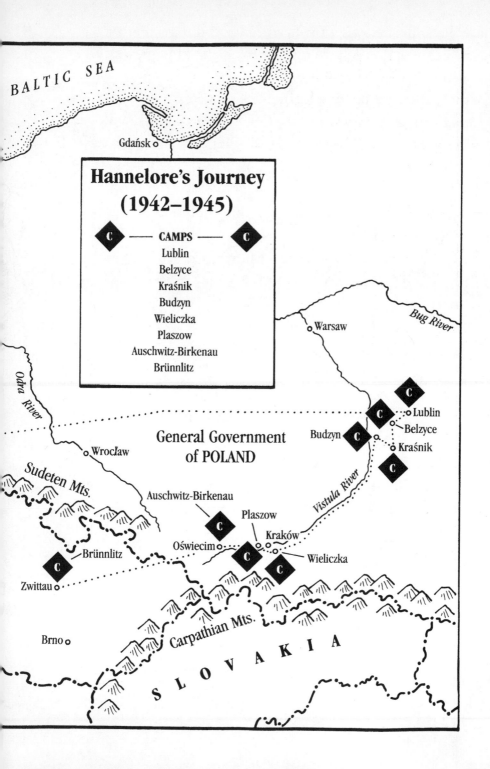

He and his followers, the Nazis, believed that all other races and cultures were inferior to them. This **prejudice** against other people was deadly. Over years, Hitler ordered the **extermination** of millions of people. Since Jews were the main target of the Nazis, two out of every three Jewish people in Europe were killed. In all, 6 million Jewish people died. This mass murder is called the Holocaust.

After years of suffering during the Holocaust, Hannelore Wolff was able to escape the horrible conditions of the concentration camps because of Oskar Schindler. Schindler owned a factory where Jewish laborers worked without pay. He profited from the war. However, Schindler grew disgusted with the cruelties inflicted on Jewish people. When orders came to transfer a group of Jewish prisoners who worked for him to death camps, he claimed that he needed them for his factory. He paid large amounts of money to save a group of his workers that was deported to Auschwitz, one of the deadliest concentration camps. He risked his wealth and his own safety and saved nearly 1,500 Jewish people during the Holocaust. Wolff was one of them.

Wolff survived and married a fellow Jewish prisoner, Bernhard Hillman. Together, the Hillmans relocated to America in 1947. Although her experiences in the Holocaust happened more than sixty years ago, she continues to speak publicly about her struggle. She believes that the story of the Holocaust must be told over and over "so it may never happen again."

Key Concepts

prejudice *n.* hatred and hostility toward a certain race or people not based on reason or experience

extermination *n.* complete destruction

prologue

"We are going to Brünnlitz, to Oskar Schindler's camp!"

I recall the shouts of joy that filled the **barrack** at Plaszow. But the terrible place where I now stand is not that **hoped-for refuge**. It is Auschwitz.

This place is different than any of the other camps I had been in. I watch prisoners pass before **an SS man** in a black uniform. He holds a leather whip in his white-gloved hand, waving it left and right, as if brushing flies away. His thin lips crimp into a smile while his eyes dart from one prisoner to another.

Not a word is said. The line to the left soon swells with elderly people and small children. A girl walking alongside me explains what it means: "People in the left line are **doomed** to die."

We have been deceived. Brünnlitz is far away. I already know some things about Auschwitz. It cannot get any worse

....

barrack building that was used as a prison
hoped-for refuge safe place that I hoped to go to
an SS man a soldier
doomed going

than this. I wait for the shooting to start, but nothing happens. Only children crying and mothers wailing, running after the young ones in the left line.

We, the three hundred women who were supposed to go to Brünnlitz, stand apart from the others. It is my hope that there is a mistake and that soon we will be loaded back on the train to go to our real destination. The music still plays, one waltz after another. I **break into tears**.

"There is no need to cry." The girl next to me **is emphatic**. "Oskar Schindler will get us out of here. You don't know him as well as we do. He will do anything for us."

"I wish I could believe you," I answer through my tears. "How can he get us out of *this* place?"

....

break into tears begin to cry
is emphatic speaks very seriously

chapter one

Since Hitler had come to power, it was dangerous for Jews to walk on public streets. In spite of the risk we walked along a tree-lined avenue in a suburb of Berlin, **the ever-present yellow Stars of David** sewn to our jackets.

Every now and then we stopped to admire spring flowers sprouting just above the ground. I especially admired the crocuses and daffodils, which reminded me of home. Irma, the tallest of us, was more interested in finding something to eat than looking at flowers, while Kaethe, the plump redhead, wanted adventure more than anything else.

This particular day Kaethe had come up with an idea. She knew of an ice-cream parlor where one could get a cone without a **ration card**.

"We've been cooped up at school too long," she said. "All we do is study. It drives me crazy! We should have more fun."

....

the ever-present yellow Stars of David and all of us had yellow stars that showed we were Jewish

ration card card given to people by the government during wartime that allowed them to get food

I shook my head. "Fun, is that all you can think about? Terrible things are happening to Jews. We should not even be on this street. They might take us away **on one of those transports**."

Kaethe paid little attention to what I had to say. She wanted ice cream. But there was still the matter of the yellow stars sewn to our clothes. No shopkeeper would serve us if he knew who we were. To Kaethe it was a minor problem. She showed us that by draping a shawl over the star it would be completely hidden. Not wanting to spoil her fun, I gave in.

Something else was troubling me that day. It had been over a month since I'd last heard from Mama and Papa. It wasn't like them to not write. Dear God, what if they had been deported? But for now I put aside my fears. Kaethe was right: What could possibly happen if we covered up the star?

We had not gone very far when two boys in the uniform of the Hitler Youth came around a corner. They were younger than we were, barely teens themselves. We tried hurrying past them, but the taller boy held up a hand and said, "We have not seen you around here before. Where are you from?"

Before we could answer, he invited us to come to a parade that night. To assure us how special this parade was, he added, "The **Führer** himself will be there!"

I felt my legs **buckling under me** from fear. "See what you got us into," I whispered angrily. "What should we do now?"

"Start giggling, Hannelore," Kaethe said. "Pretend you are

---

on one of those transports and bring us to a concentration camp

Führer Leader of the country (in German)

buckling under me shaking; weakening

a moron. You too, Irma."

The second boy looked closely at our shawls. "Why are you wearing those silly things?" he asked.

Before I could think of an answer, he pulled at my shawl, exposing the yellow star.

"Look at this!" he shouted. "*Jews,* hiding their identity. You filthy swine, we will teach you a lesson you'll never forget! Let's take them to **Gestapo headquarters**," he told his companion. "They will **get what is coming to them**, and we will get a medal for bringing them in."

His fist struck me in the face and bloodied my nose. I ignored the pain and bleeding. The word *Gestapo* frightened me more than my injuries.

The boy held on to my arm. He was hurting me, but I didn't let on how painful it was. When he **loosened his grip** just a little, I pulled free and shouted to my friends, "Run, *run!*"

I am not sure how we managed to get away from those boys. Perhaps they decided they had better things to do than torment girls, even Jewish girls. Somehow we reached the gate to our school and ran inside. To make us feel better, Kaethe brought out a bar of chocolate her parents had sent. Before long things returned to normal. We changed clothes and talked about the young teacher who had come to lecture us on the poems of Rainer Maria Rilke, my favorite poet.

Kaethe began teasing me. "He **had eyes only for you**, Hannelore. The way you recited 'The Lute,' that was special.

....

Gestapo headquarters the German police who are controlled by Nazis

get what is coming to them get what they deserve; be punished

loosened his grip stopped holding my arm

had eyes only for you was only interested in you

He stared at your lips throughout the entire poem."

Irma laughed. **My face turned beet red.** Yes, I did **have a crush on** the teacher. If only Kaethe wouldn't tease me about it so much.

"I wish I had your dreamy eyes," Kaethe continued. "Maybe then boys would look at me, too."

It was time to go down to the study hall. The room was crowded, which usually didn't bother me, but today I found it hard to concentrate. The encounter with the two Hitler Youth had troubled me more than I would admit to anyone. I decided I would be better able to concentrate on my studies in our room and returned there. **Before long I was completely absorbed in** my work. Then a girl entered.

"Mail," she said in a singsong voice, placing letters on the table.

I looked through the stack, picking up the one letter addressed to me. Thank God, a letter from Mama! Hastily, I tore open the envelope and began to read:

Dearest Hannelore,

I am sorry I didn't write to you sooner, but I have been terribly worried. Six weeks ago your papa was taken to Buchenwald, a concentration camp near Weimar. He was on his way home from work, riding his bicycle, when the Gestapo stopped him and took him to their headquarters. The next day, when I inquired about where he was and asked if I could bring him a change of clothes,

....

My face turned beet red. I looked very embarrassed.

have a crush on like

Before long I was completely absorbed in Soon, I was only thinking about

I was told he had already left the city and wouldn't need the clothes. You can imagine how concerned and upset I have been since. Day after day I prayed for his safe return.

Yesterday the postman brought a letter and a small box postmarked "Buchenwald." The letter said the following: "Martin Wolff died of unknown causes on March 14, 1942. **Urn** *contains his ashes."*

Hannelore, your papa is dead.

Nausea overwhelmed me, and I barely made it to the bathroom down the hall. *"They murdered him!"* I cried. *"They murdered Papa!* Why doesn't someone stop this killing? Dear God, *doesn't anyone care?"*

Sweat and tears **streamed** down my face. The room began to whirl. *"They murdered Papa!"* I shrieked again. "How can they get away with this?"

I sobbed and sobbed as I staggered back to my room and fell on the bed. The next thing I remember was someone leaning over me.

"You left the study hall," Kaethe said, "so I came up to— Hannelore, what's wrong? What happened?"

"Here." I handed her the letter. "I told you I was worried about my parents, but you **made light of it** and called me names!"

I began crying again. After finishing the letter, Kaethe also cried, and she held me for a few moments as the sobs threatened

....

Urn *The small vase*
Nausea overwhelmed me I suddenly felt very sick
streamed quickly flowed
made light of it acted like it was not important

to shatter my body.

Finally I stopped sobbing. Kaethe remained sitting next to me. I began to talk, telling my friend why I believed Mama and Papa had not left Germany before it was too late. "Papa made himself believe he would be safe. After all, he **served** in the war in 1918, where he was wounded and **decorated**. On the night the Nazis burned **our synagogue**, Papa came home; all the other men were sent to Buchenwald."

I could never forget that horrible night.

It was November 9, 1938. The Germans called it *Kristallnacht*—the night of broken glass—because not only did they burn our synagogue, they broke the windows in Jewish-owned businesses. I told Kaethe what it was like when Nazis in brown shirts and black boots stormed through our front door, ordering us out.

"You can't imagine the kind of foul language they used," I said, "while we stood to watch the synagogue burn. It was awful." Afterward we could no longer go to school; it too had been burned. Besides, from then on Jewish children all over Germany were not allowed to attend public schools. Papa found a Jewish school in Cologne for Wolfgang and Selly, my younger brothers, eleven and twelve at the time. The boys had to live in **an orphanage there** in order to attend. Thank God he didn't have to worry about Rosel and Hildegard, my older sisters. Both had left home a few years ago to work as mother's helpers for a Jewish family in the city of Fulda. In 1939 Rosel was able

....

served was a soldier

decorated given medals for being a good soldier

our synagogue the place where we worshipped God

an orphanage there a home for children without parents

to leave for England. Hildegard went to Palestine in 1940. A year later we received a letter from the Red Cross, telling us Hildegard was living in Jerusalem. Papa and Mama were happy about that, and wished all their children could leave, but that was not possible now. Soon after Papa had taken care of the boys, he showed me a picture of Dr. Frenkel's Boarding School for Jewish Girls in a suburb of Berlin. He assured me I would be happy there.

"It . . . was the last time I saw him," I told Kaethe. "I wrote every week telling him how much the garden here reminded me of our garden at home in Aurich. But I missed the small forest behind our house, the one with the brook running through it. It wasn't really a brook—just a trickle of water—but we called it that. Wolfgang, Selly, and I played our favorite games there, games about the war made up from the stories Papa told us. We would pretend to be shot, and then, when confronted by a Russian **bayonet**, we would recite the prayer: "Hear, O Israel . . ."

The news of Papa's murder spread quickly. Classmates came to my room with small gifts. Spread out on my quilt were sugar cubes wrapped in cellophane, small pieces of chocolate, cookies, and wildflowers from the garden—gifts only children know how to appreciate. Their kindness **touched me**. Surely the food had been saved over a long time, for **delicacies like these were hard to come by**. When the dinner bell rang, they all

....

bayonet gun with a knife attached to it

touched me made me feel like I was loved

delicacies like these were hard to come by special foods like these were hard to get

urged me to come with them, but I could not. The idea of not having a father anymore . . . It was all too **raw**. I wanted, needed to be alone. So many memories to confront . . . It would soon be **Passover**, but Papa would never **preside over the feast** again, never sing the songs of freedom or offer gratitude for our people having **come out of Egypt**. Papa, with his beautiful voice, always on key.

Hannelore Wolff, sixteen years old, 1940.

---

raw new and painful
Passover a special Jewish holiday
preside over the feast say the prayers for the holiday meal
come out of Egypt escaped from slavery

My eyes came to rest on the bookshelf. The first week at school, when I was terribly homesick, books had been my **solace**. I picked up a thin volume of Rilke's poems. Papa's artistic lettering was on the **flyleaf**.

October 16, 1940
To Hannelore,
on the occasion of your birthday.
With love from Mama and Papa

The slender volume fell open to page 77 and a favorite poem called "Before the Summer Rain." Reciting from memory I heard myself chanting the lines:

"Suddenly in the park from all the green,
one knows not what,
but something real is gone . . ."

Drawn to the simplicity of the poem, I recited it with intense emotion. The words had a deeply personal meaning. Putting the book back in its place, I next lovingly ran my hands over the volumes of Heinrich Heine and was reminded of the essay contest that had earned me these works. When I was preparing to move to the boarding school, Mama suggested I take only a few of my books to Berlin. "But, Mama," I had argued, "I need them all."

....

solace comfort, relief
flyleaf first page of the book
Drawn to Because I liked

I walked over to the window. The chirping birds nestling under the eaves of the roof usually delighted me. Today I did not even turn my head. The thought of Papa and how he might have died **tormented me**. If only I could be certain they had not tortured him . . .

I cried again as if my heart would break, soon knowing that, indeed, it had.

It always amazed me how three girls living in a tiny attic room stayed friends. But that's how it had been from the start. We teased one another a lot, but there was no viciousness to it. Sometimes I made fun of Kaethe's doll collection, to which she replied, "I am not **letting go of my childhood** yet. At sixteen I can still pretend."

Both Kaethe and Irma had come from small towns in Westphalia. Up until Hitler's rise to power they had happily **coexisted** with children in public school. Now the laws of the **Third Reich** didn't allow Jewish students to attend public schools. Since there was no Jewish school in their town, they, too, had come to Berlin to Dr. Frenkel's boarding school.

Irma was often homesick. She missed her young brothers. But still, she loved having fun, entertaining us with exotic dances. Kaethe was practical. "If it weren't for Hitler's laws," she proclaimed, "I would have been stuck in Lingen for the rest of my life."

Kaethe was like that. She could turn a bad situation into

....

tormented me caused me great pain
letting go of my childhood ready to grow up
coexisted gone to school
Third Reich German government under Adolf Hitler

a good one.

When the girls returned from dinner, I had **recovered some control of my emotions**. I needed little encouragement from them to talk about my childhood, about the ivy-covered house we had lived in, in Aurich, Ostfriesland—the house with the secret passageways. A faint smile creased my face when I talked about the storks nesting on top of the chimney and how as children we believed the story told us, that storks bring babies. But the best part was the friends I played hopscotch with, and hide-and-seek, and all the other games of childhood. And how it all changed when Hitler came to power.

The speeches Hitler made were mostly about his hatred for Jews. We told Papa of our fears, how afraid we were. He assured us that all this would blow over very soon. Yet oftentimes I saw him and my uncles having serious discussions.

Soon Wolfgang's and Selly's best friends didn't just stop coming to play, they repeated the **slogans** Hitler used in his speeches and what their parents, who now wore the uniform of the Brownshirts, the Nazi militiamen, told them to say. Carl, who had been Wolfgang's best friend, shouted from across the street, "My father belongs to the **SA**. He says he can do whatever he wants to Jews and no one will stop him."

"Can you imagine how we felt when he said that?" I asked them. "Wolfgang tried to **reason with** him, reminding him that they were best friends, but Carl didn't listen."

Kaethe had similar stories about her little village: "One

....

recovered some control of my emotions stopped crying
slogans mean and hateful phrases
SA group that acts like an army for the government
reason with talk to

day we were friends, the next day they **boycotted** us. Nazis in brown shirts and black boots paraded around Father's sawmill, making sure no one entered. A few months from the time they first appeared, we were ordered to leave the village and our sawmill was given to a Nazi."

I told Kaethe and Irma about the time when a German friend of Papa's came one evening, after dark. He warned Papa to leave Germany as soon as he could. That was all he would say. But Papa still didn't listen.

"I fought for Germany," he told the man. "I am a decorated war veteran. They wouldn't harm me."

And yet in 1940 Mama and Papa, along with all the Jews of Aurich and of the entire region called Ostfriesland, were deported. They were no longer allowed to live there. Having to leave most of their possessions behind, they opted to go to Weimar, where Mama's married sister lived and where Grandmother Henriette, her mother, wanted to go. Not that they could have chosen any other place—permission to live in other cities was limited.

Suddenly the undulating sound of sirens interrupted us. "**Air raid!** To the cellar!" the housemother cried as she ran from floor to floor.

"I am not going," I said. "Everyone will ask questions. I can't **face** that, not now. Go without me."

But Kaethe and Irma would not **hear of leaving me**. We

....

boycotted stopped talking to
Air raid! Planes have started dropping bombs!
face deal with; handle
hear of leaving me leave me alone

crawled under the beds as a **fireball** exploded in the sky.

"It might have been wiser for you to go to the cellar," I whispered.

"And leave you up here alone?" Irma said.

She had barely finished her words when the thunder of another crash made us **recoil**. The wait was unbearable. Bomb after bomb exploded all around us. I was certain we would be hit at any moment.

Then, as suddenly as it began, it stopped. Still, we remained under the beds until another siren officially announced the end of the raid.

....

fireball bomb
recoil jump with fear

BEFORE YOU MOVE ON...

1. **Author's Style** The prologue takes place in Auschwitz, but the author starts the story in Berlin. Why do you think the author does this?

2. **Summarize** What was happening in Germany when Hannelore was growing up? What could Hannelore no longer do?

LOOK AHEAD Read to page 45 to see what brave decision Hannelore made.

chapter two

A few weeks later while studying in my room another letter arrived:

Weimar, April 12th, 1942
Dearest Hannelore,
*It has been four weeks since Papa's ashes were brought to me and now there are new developments. The Gestapo has notified me that I am to be deported to the East—**whatever that means**. Your brothers are still in Cologne, but they, too, got the same notice. We are to **present ourselves at** the animal hall in Weimar on May 8th and are allowed to bring only one suitcase and a **knapsack**. All else is to be left behind. I **am at a loss of** what to take, not knowing how long we'll be gone. How I wish Papa were here! I miss him so. Do what you can to save yourself, my dearest child. When all this is over we*

....

whatever that means *I am not sure what that means*
present ourselves at *go to*
knapsack *small bag*
am at a loss of *do not know*

will be together again. Remember that no matter how far
away I am from you, I will always be near.
    Your loving
    Mama

I thought about all the bad things I had heard about deportation. It meant being in labor camps, where life was difficult, where there was never enough food, and where beatings took place. How could Mama **stand up to that**? And what about Wolfgang and Selly? They were so young.

Only a few nights ago I dreamt about Papa sitting at the **head of** the table on Passover night. He sang all the familiar songs of freedom. In the dream I smelled the chicken soup, the stewed carrots and prunes. At the end of the feast it seemed as if Papa was trying to tell me something, but I could not hear him. . . .

Rain came down in torrents, but I paid little attention to it. I grabbed my coat and ran aimlessly into the street, trying to **sort out** Mama's news. There was no letup in the rain as I walked farther and farther away from the school. Raindrops gathered at the tip of my nose; my hair clung to my face in wet strings. Finally the sole of one shoe came loose, and I stumbled over a branch that had fallen in my path. I turned around and went back. Not bothering to change into dry clothes when I reached my room, I sat down to write a letter.

....

stand up to that *survive there; live there*
head of most important seat at; end of
sort out carefully think about; understand

To Gestapo Headquarters in Weimar,

    I hereby apply for permission to travel from Berlin to Weimar. My mother, Karoline Wolff, and my brothers, Wolfgang and Selly Wolff, are being deported on May 8th, from Weimar. I wish to **accompany** *them.*

    Hannelore Wolff

"Who are you writing to?" Kaethe asked.

"You already know the answer," I said sourly. "You've been **looking over my shoulder** the whole time. I know what you're going to say, that I should think about this carefully. Well, I *have* thought about it. I must go with my mother to wherever that may be. I have to protect her and my brothers. Anyway, sooner or later they will put us *all* on transports, deport all of us."

Kaethe **was visibly alarmed**. "Hannelore, read your mother's letter again. She asked you to save yourself! You don't seem to know what saving yourself means. It means staying right here. Don't think for a minute that the Nazis will let Hannelore Wolff stay with her mother and brothers because she volunteered to come along on this transport. Families get separated when deported. Haven't you heard?"

Kaethe raised her voice for emphasis. "You don't seem to realize what you are **letting yourself in for**."

I wanted to hug Kaethe; I knew she meant well, but she brushed me away. She was too upset.

"Tell her, Irma," Kaethe said in a raspy voice. "Maybe she'll

---

accompany go with
looking over my shoulder reading what I was writing
was visibly alarmed looked terrified
letting yourself in for doing

listen to you."

"Kaethe is right," Irma agreed. "We can't let you do this. Give me that letter."

She sprang from her bed trying to wrestle the letter out of my hand. I ran from the room crying. Irma's voice trailed after me. "By the time the Nazis get around to us, the war may be over."

After that the waiting for the daily mail delivery began. May 8th was not far away, and still the Gestapo had not answered my letter. To **relieve the tension**, I often walked in the school's garden. On one of my walks I saw Kaethe coming toward me waving a letter. I tore at the envelope, opening it swiftly. It was from the Gestapo and gave me permission to use the train from Berlin to Weimar for the purpose of being deported. The letter went on with **formalities of** how to obtain a ticket for a Jewish person.

I looked up at Kaethe. "Oh my God, what have I done?"

My travel permit was issued for May 2nd, in two days. It was time for me to begin sorting out my possessions.

"Keep my books till I get back. I will take only the Rilke poems," I said. "Do you think my saddle shoes will fit one of you? You have always admired them. And here, take my gym clothes. I won't need them."

That night, sitting on our beds, we talked about the future. Irma **composed an ad** we would place in the *Berliner*

....

relieve the tension try to stay calm

formalities of instructions on

composed an ad wrote an advertisement so we could find each other after the war that

Rundschau, a **widely read paper**.

"We'll use last names only. saying, Reunion for Gruenstein, Wolff, and Helfen taking place at Wangenheimstrasse 36. Berlin, Grünewald. Bring amusing stories."

I held her hand tightly. "Our Irma, funny to the end."

"Funny, only because there is nothing else we can do. How else **to cope with an insane world**?"

Would we see one another again? The question **nagged at** us, yet we dared not say it aloud.

I left Berlin two days later at eight o'clock in the morning.

....

widely read paper newspaper many people read

to cope with an insane world can we survive in a place where people are being punished for no reason

nagged at bothered

chapter three

Dressed in a white blouse, blue corduroy skirt, and matching jacket, I boarded the train. I could have been any young girl going home for spring vacation had it not been for the yellow Star of David sewn to my jacket. People stared but said nothing. Ticket in hand, I soon found the right **compartment**. As I took my seat the couple next to me moved away. Across from me sat two soldiers and a boy in a Hitler Youth uniform. More people entered the compartment, and before long the whistle blew as the train began to move, slowly **winding its way** through the maze of tracks at Hauptbahnhof, Berlin's busiest railroad station.

So began my trip home. I knew that this trip was different from any I had ever taken. Left behind was school, my friends— my whole life. Ahead, a future over which I had no control.

Sitting quietly, I listened to the conversations around me. A young mother with a baby **confided** to the woman

....

compartment place to sit on the train
winding its way moving
confided told a secret

accompanying her that her husband had joined the **party**—and wasn't it marvelous that they were given one of the apartments Jews **had to vacate**? "It's completely furnished," she added.

A chill passed down my spine. In a week's time some party member would live in our house.

Not to be outdone, the other blonde leaned over to tell her companion what was to be a secret. "Horst has a new assignment. We're moving to Poland, near one of those camps. He said we will get a lot of special privileges."

My attention shifted to the soldiers, who were playing a noisy game of cards. When the game ended, they began to sing the party song, the refrain repeating itself after every verse. I was familiar with the song. A man named Horst Wessel had written the words: *"When Jewish blood spurts from our knives, things will go twice as well."*

I was afraid to look up for fear of being **harassed**, but nothing happened. When the singing ended, everyone began to eat. I took out a cheese sandwich and an apple. Early that morning I had gone down to the school kitchen to ask the cook if he had something to give me for the journey.

The train moved past fields and meadows. Marigolds and cornflowers blanketed the countryside. Now and then a peasant guided his herd of cows toward a watering hole. The tranquility of the scene did little to put me at ease. I tried preparing myself for the reunion with Mama, thinking of what I would say to console her. If only Papa had listened to his friend Mr.

....

party Nazi political party
had to vacate were forced to leave
Not to be outdone Wanting to sound important
harassed yelled at; attacked

Wasserman, who had **emigrated** with his family to Argentina while there was still time.

"Argentina," Papa had said. "It's at the end of the world."

If only Papa had listened.

The voice of a vendor selling tea, coffee, and mineral water rang through the corridor. My throat was dry from the stale air in the compartment, and I longed for a glass of mineral water but didn't want to **chance being refused**. When the young woman with the baby asked for coffee with cream and sugar, the vendor grew angry, telling her that such luxuries were reserved for men fighting **at the front**.

A bell rang, and two uniformed SS men entered the compartment. "We are looking for Hannelore Wolff," they said gruffly. I sprang to my feet and showed them my travel permit. I was very frightened, with visions of being arrested and pulled off the train before I reached Weimar. Mama would never know what had happened to me. But after checking my papers, one of them dismissed me with a grunt.

The other passengers paid little attention to me, and having no one to talk to only heightened my loneliness. After a while I picked up a memory book the class had given me as a going-away present. Each of the girls had written a poem. I felt inspired by the more original ones, but even the simpler sayings made me think about the camaraderie that had existed among us. I struggled to hold back tears; I couldn't let that happen, not here.

....

emigrated moved out of the country

chance being refused be told I could not have one because I was Jewish

at the front in the war

The hours dragged by, but finally the conductor announced, "Next station, Weimar."

The school had sent a telegram letting Mama know when I was arriving. Mama was waiting on the platform, as beautiful as I remembered her. Shiny black hair, a flawless complexion glowing like a freshly ripened peach. But now there was a look, a **wary** expression that had never been there before. Mama held me in her arms and made a feeble attempt to smile. I sobbed uncontrollably into the folds of her black dress.

After a minute I wiped the tears and said, "I often think Papa will come back. That maybe they made a mistake."

"I wish that were so," Mama replied, "but that is not the reality of it."

People began to gather around us, staring at our yellow stars. We hurried to get away as quickly as possible. **Our departure was accompanied by insults.** One man followed us clear across the tracks shouting, "Germany will soon be *judenrein*"— free of Jews.

As we walked along a group of prisoners in gray-and-blue-striped burlap uniforms with numbers stenciled on their backs passed by. I had never, ever seen such **emaciated** faces. I was certain they were from Buchenwald, only an hour away from here.

Buchenwald, where Papa had been murdered.

We were halfway home when, unable to contain myself any longer, I asked Mama how it happened that Papa was arrested.

....

wary careful, distrustful

Our departure was accompanied by insults. People called us bad names as we left the station.

emaciated thin, skinny

She started from the beginning, telling of Papa's assigned job with a potato dealer. He had to fill large burlap sacks with potatoes from early morning till night. Since Jews were not allowed to use public transportation and the dealer was far away, he rode his bicycle. The knee injury he had sustained in the Great War made walking difficult.

One day as he rode home the Gestapo stopped him and asked to see his permit. He didn't know that a permit was needed for riding a bicycle.

"Couldn't he have **paid a fine**?" I asked.

"Don't you see, it was an excuse to arrest him. When he didn't come home, I was frantic. But I couldn't go out to look for him because **of the curfew**."

Mama went on to tell me how the next morning she had gone to the place where Papa worked. That was when she found out about his arrest.

"I begged the potato dealer to **intercede**, to tell the Gestapo that Papa was needed, but he didn't want to get involved. I went to Gestapo headquarters asking permission to bring Papa a change of clothes and the special bandages he needed for his knee.

"The Gestapo refused to hear me out. 'He doesn't need anything. We already told you that. Go home.'"

It hurt me so much to remind Mama of these terrible events, but in order to make sense of it, I had to know.

"It is beyond my understanding that the Gestapo has so

....

paid a fine given them money as a punishment instead of being arrested

of the curfew people were not allowed to be outside of their homes after a certain time every night

intercede do something to help Papa

much power!" I cried out. "They can grab a man off the street, send him to Buchenwald . . . and *kill him*. Is that how they repay a man for fighting their Great War, for being wounded and suffering from the pain all of his life!"

Just then as we were walking along I was reminded of our ivy-covered home in Aurich. How I longed to see it one more time to remind me of the happy hours I had spent there. I **visualized** the house now, with its massive front door and the weather vane perched on top of the chimney—a circle with a pierced arrow through the center. When I was little, Grandmother Rosette told me about weather vanes and how they worked as lightning rods. And I wanted to see the lilac tree, imagining it full of blossoms. I had always liked the fragrance of lilacs. Besides, the tree always bloomed around Mama's birthday. It was almost that time again, only now Mama lived in Weimar in **crammed quarters**. There was no lilac tree, and Papa was not here to sing his songs of love.

Memories **flooded through** my mind. I could almost see Papa's shell collection displayed in the entry hall and the portraits of Grandmother Rosette and Grandfather Wolff dressed in the fashion of the day hanging side by side. I was only two years old when Grandfather Wolff died, but I fondly remembered Grandmother Rosette. I visited her every summer in Marienhafe. Two years ago when Jews were not allowed to live in Marienhafe anymore, my grandmother moved to **an old-age home**. That home had been evacuated to a camp

....

visualized thought about; could see
crammed quarters a small house
flooded through filled
an old-age home a place where older people lived

called Theresienstadt. We never heard from her again.

Finally Mama and I arrived at our destination. It was a long walk, especially for me since I was carrying my suitcase. The house we stopped at was a square, unattractive building. It was dark inside and very quiet. Mama and I walked through the long hall, arriving at the last door, and there, grabbing the door handle when they heard a key turning, were my brothers Wolfgang and Selly.

It was wonderful to see them again. They had arrived from Cologne only a few days ago and were no longer the little boys I remembered. They had not even had their **bar mitzvahs** yet when we parted. I could not believe these tall, lanky young men were my brothers. Selly's hair was still blond, while Wolfgang resembled Mama. He had her jet-black hair. **Our childhood flashed before me**: the games we had played, the tricks we had performed with worms and other insects to frighten our friends. It might as well have been a lifetime ago, the way everything had changed.

"What about your bar mitzvahs?" I asked them. "You never answered my letters. It must have been hard for you without us there on such an important day. Papa tried to get a travel permit each time, but you know what happened. The authorities refused him."

"It was the same for all the boys," Wolfgang replied. "What should have been a special occasion turned into a sad day."

I knew that Mama was happy to see us together, and when

....

bar mitzvahs important religious ceremonies for 13-year-old Jewish boys

Our childhood flashed before me I suddenly remembered times when we were children

Hannelore's brothers, Wolfgang (left) and Selly (right).

Selly remarked that I looked like a **"real girl"** now, even Mama smiled. We talked about our experiences in air-raid shelters, friends who had already been deported, and what our teachers had been like. Then it was time for me to go upstairs to **pay my respects** to Grandmother Henriette, who lived on the floor above.

....

"real girl" grown woman
pay my respects say hello

The curtains **had not been drawn**, allowing the late-afternoon light to illuminate the room. Grandmother Henriette sat in a high-back armchair, her feet resting on a footstool. She wore the same hairdo as always, with a net over it, but now her hair was completely gray.

I curtsied, as was expected of me, and planted a kiss on my grandmother's hand, barely touching the skin. "You've grown," she said. "Just like your brothers."

"Can you imagine, Grandmother," I replied, "Selly told me I look like a real girl now!"

That brought a faint smile to the old woman's face. Grandmother said she remembered the wild games I had played with the boys, climbing trees as well as they did. "That's **all behind you now**," she said. "Your papa is gone, and you are going to be deported. Writing to the Gestapo to ask permission to go with your mama was a brave thing to do, Hannelore."

The mention of Papa again brought tears to my face. Grandmother Henriette, who had always been strict and formal with her grandchildren, now opened both arms to comfort me.

It was getting dark. I rose to close the curtains and light a lamp. That's when I noticed the deep lines on my grandmother's face and saw **how much she had aged**. She would be alone after our deportation.

"Will they let you stay here after we leave?" I asked innocently.

"Probably not, child. I have no **illusions** about my future.

....

had not been drawn were open
all behind you now in the past
how much she had aged how old and tired she looked
illusions false hope

My turn to be deported will come soon enough. I've wondered why they are letting me stay for now. Why not let me go with you?"

"The Gestapo is unpredictable," I replied. "Wolfgang and Selly got deportation notices, I did not. I can't figure it out."

I could see my grandmother was getting tired of this conversation, and anyway, I wanted to be with Mama and the boys.

Mama was sitting in her room when I came down. The massive ebony furniture was gone, left behind in Aurich, but the room was **spotless**. Mama was a wonderful housekeeper. The drapes were **hand-embroidered** by Mama herself. She had brought them along, and they looked freshly laundered.

"I have something to show you," Mama whispered, taking a small, sharp-edged box from the sideboard drawer. "This box . . ." For a moment she could not speak. "Papa's ashes. They came with the letter from Buchenwald."

I held on to the box with both hands, wanting to say something but having trouble **shaping the words**. Tears rolled freely down my face when I **blurted out**, "Papa, I will never forget you as long as I am alive, and I will never forgive the Germans who did this to you! I promise, one day, when the Nazis are gone, we will return and give you a proper Jewish burial. *Papa, I don't know what to do without you!* But Mama needs me, and I have to be strong. I ask God why he let this happen to you—"

....

spotless very clean
hand-embroidered made by hand
shaping the words thinking of what to say
blurted out said without thinking

"Hannelore, what kind of talk is that?" Mama exclaimed. "We do not question **God's will**. It has been a long, exhausting day. That's the only excuse I have for you!"

"I am sorry Mama. I didn't mean it that way. Please . . . forgive me."

I turned toward my brothers, who had now joined us in Mama's room, and wondered out loud why the Gestapo had bothered to send Papa's ashes to us. They didn't do that when **Frau** Guttman was killed in Ravensbrück, that awful concentration camp for women. Her ashes were not returned.

No one could understand how the Gestapo worked and how they operated. **Power had gone to their heads**, and they did whatever they wanted to do.

I shared the room with Mama that night. We looked through photographs and mementos well past midnight.

"Do you remember this one?" Mama said, glancing at a photo of Selly at the age of four, posing for a beauty contest. How handsome he was with his blond locks. He looks like a girl here."

There were more pictures of the boys on their first day of school, and one of me as well . . . pictures of Papa in his army uniform from the Great War and a last picture of him having to sell potatoes. Mama buried her face into a pillow as she looked at it. When I tried to console her, she simply said, "Let me be. I cry to relieve my pain."

During the night, when neither of us could sleep, Mama told

....

God's will why God does certain things
Frau Mrs. (in German)
Power had gone to their heads The Gestapo had become very powerful and self-important

me how grateful she was to have me by her side in the difficult times that lay ahead. But perhaps, she said, it would have been wiser for me to stay in Berlin.

"They might have let you stay a few more months, a year. A lot can happen in a year. Don't be fooled, Hannelore. There are worse things than labor camps and hunger. For now we are going to the East, or so they tell us. We may well end up in a labor camp first, but there are concentration camps in the East, too."

"I know," I said. "I have heard how bad concentration camps in Poland are. All the more reason for me to be with you and the boys. We'll face it together."

Early the next morning I knocked on Wolfgang and Selly's door. They had never been neat, but what I saw now was **utter chaos**. Everything was **strewn** around—games, clothes, books, skates.

"I am surprised you found room to sleep," I said. "You can take only one suitcase and a knapsack. There is enough here to fill two trunks."

"What difference does anything make?" Wolfgang replied **with an air of resignation**.

So young, and already full of despair, I thought. How does one get ready for deportation? My own attempt to pack **didn't get far** either. Mama believed I was having a hard time leaving my possessions behind.

"You know me better than that," I told her. "It's not the

....

utter chaos a very big mess
strewn thrown, scattered
with an air of resignation sounding hopeless
didn't get far was not successful

things I have to leave behind, it's . . . **the idea**. First they kill Papa, then they throw us out of our home, ordering us to leave behind everything that rightfully belongs to us. If only Papa were here!"

"Even he couldn't help us now. He would be as powerless as we are. Sixty million Germans against five hundred thousand Jews. Think, Hannelore, think."

Mama was right, of course: We *were* powerless. I began at once to pack, counting out seven pairs of underwear, four blouses, shoes, sweaters, and so on, until the suitcase was filled. I put the slim volume of the Rilke poems between a nightgown and a blouse, and then squeezed the suitcase shut.

....

the idea what they are forcing us to do that bothers me

BEFORE YOU MOVE ON...

1. **Conclusions** What risk did Hannelore take by joining her family?

2. **Inference** Reread pages 44–45. Hannelore said, "It's not the things I have to leave behind, it's . . . the idea." What does this tell you about her?

LOOK AHEAD Read pages 46–63 to find out what life was like in the ghetto.

chapter four

All too soon May 8th arrived. With knapsacks strapped to our backs and suitcases packed to the limit, we **set out**.

Grandmother Henriette stood in the doorway waving, a handkerchief pressed to her eyes. Mama **let a groan escape her lips** that sounded like, *May God help us.*

It was Mama's forty-third birthday. In times past we would have **serenaded** her, brought her flowers from the meadow, perhaps recited a poem. But on this day, May 8, 1942, the day of our deportation, there was no birthday celebration.

On our way we encountered a flurry of people going to market. A boy delivering newspapers raced through the streets on his bicycle. The Mueller's Bakery truck darted in and out of streets and alleyways, the driver calling, "Fresh rolls, fresh rolls!'

Not one person extended a greeting or a farewell wish.

The assembly place for the deportees was Weimar's

....

set out left the house
let a groan escape her lips made a sound
serenaded sang songs to

stock pen. Armed SA men guarded the entrance. Had the Nazis chosen this place to further humiliate us, to **equate Jews with animals**?

The sour smell of fear mixed with cow dung and straw was overpowering. More and more people arrived carrying suitcases. Old and young, they lined up to have their papers examined. I had never been in a stock pen before. Along the wall were individual stalls designed to hold animals, and to the side stood a large scale. Beyond that were the railroad tracks.

I saw a sign that read MEN AND BOYS TO THE LEFT, WOMEN AND GIRLS TO THE RIGHT.

Wolfgang and Selly moved to the left without looking back, while I pressed closer to Mama. Nazis shouted at everyone who entered. I worried about my brothers. They were too young to have to **fend for themselves in this hostile atmosphere**.

More and more people arrived. I recognized acquaintances but was too scared to even nod to them. Older women, barely able to lift their suitcases, were told to carry them or leave them behind. I wanted to help but was not allowed to do so. Slowly, the line began to move. All suitcases had to be opened, and SA women rummaged through them to look for valuables. Mama was told to remove her gold wedding band. She had never taken the ring off before. Then it was my turn. The same woman who had ordered Mama to take off her band rummaged around my suitcase and removed a Tyrolean sweater, one of my favorites. She also took the antique silver bracelet I was wearing. It had

....

stock pen area where animals were usually kept

equate Jews with animals make us feel like we were animals

fend for themselves in this hostile atmosphere protect themselves in this awful place

been a present from my great-uncle Nathan Schoenthal and was the only piece of jewelry I owned. I bit my lip to keep from crying out.

More lines, more orders, more confusion followed. **A strip search was ordered.** The SA woman in charge was threatening. "Take your clothes off, damned Jewess! Make it fast, I don't have all day. There are too many of you as it is."

I peeled off layer after layer of clothing with the greatest speed and stood naked, for the first time in my life, among strangers. I felt violated.

"Tell me where you hid your valuables. It will save time," the SA woman snapped.

When I told her politely that I had already handed over my bracelet, as I was told to do, she began a body search, examining **every crevice**. I had never been so disgraced.

By the time all the body searches and other formalities we had to go through were over, it was afternoon. I was very hungry and cold. But I soon forgot my own discomfort when I heard a piercing cry coming from the men's side of the hall. I was concerned for my brothers. Had they said or done something they shouldn't have?

Walking quickly as far as I dared to, I soon saw what was happening. An SA man was standing over a deportee and beating him relentlessly, dragging him around the straw-covered stall. I didn't want to look, but the wailing was so pitiful that the man was impossible to ignore.

....

A strip search was ordered. We were told to take off our clothes so that the SA could check our bodies.

every crevice every place on my body I could have hidden something of value

"Hear, O Israel," the man cried. "Hear, O Israel, the Lord our God, the Lord is One."

It was that old familiar prayer, chanted on **Shabbat** and at holiday services . . . and sometimes before dying.

The SA man continued to swing his club long after the man had fallen silent. Even from a distance I could tell he had been beaten to death. One of the **orderlies** was called.

"Out of my sight with this dog. Take him away."

"God, what have we done that you have **forsaken us**?" I uttered under my breath.

....

Shabbat the Jewish day of worship and rest
orderlies helpers, assistants
forsaken us left us to be treated so horribly

chapter five

We had spent the entire day at the stock pen, and now it was evening. A voice over the loudspeaker told us to board the train through the back doors. **Floodlights** glared overhead as we were rushed onto the platform, ordered to move faster, *faster*. When I saw Wolfgang and Selly in the crowd, I walked toward them so we could board the train together.

Mama found a seat on a bench; we sat on our suitcases. The last of the deportees had long been pushed inside, yet still the train didn't move. Lights flickered on and off. I felt **people and the walls closing in around me**. Hours later, when windows and doors had been sealed and bars laid across them, the train jerked forward and back. One final shudder, and **we were off into the unknown**. Except for the sound of the turning wheels, there was total silence.

Wolfgang and Selly sat together, knees drawn up, looking

....

Floodlights Bright lights

people and the walls closing in around me very crowded and scared

we were off into the unknown the train began to move, but we did not know where it was going

frightened. To calm myself, I closed my eyes, **as though I were pulling shades down on the world**.

When streaks of morning light filtered into the compartment, I stood up and rubbed my cramped legs. Mama was way over on the other side of the compartment, and since I would have to step and crawl over people to get to her, I simply waved.

After people started waking and we were able to move closer to one another, my brothers and I took a Thermos of tea and sandwiches from our knapsacks and had breakfast with Mama. Food **lifted our spirits**. We'd had nothing to eat since we had left the house in Weimar.

"Where do you think we are?" Wolfgang asked between bites.

Since I didn't know, I asked a young man sitting next to us. He was about my age and hadn't said a word to anyone.

"We are in Poland," he answered.

I offered him some tea, but he declined, saying he was too upset to eat or drink. His name was Erich Neuman. There had been an incident at the Weimar railroad station. His father had been beaten. Erich didn't know **the outcome**; he had been ordered onto the train.

As the day unfolded we went past fields where farmers worked and wildflowers bloomed. Every now and then a farmer in a horse-drawn cart drove by and stared at the passing train, at the faces pressed against its windows.

Late in the afternoon the steam engine began hissing and

....

as though I were pulling shades down on the world
pretending that I was not on the train

lifted our spirits made us feel a little better

the outcome what happened to his father

brakes were applied. Within minutes the train came to a full stop. After the iron bars had been lifted, we were ordered to get out.

"Alles raus" was the phrase used, meaning "every*thing* out," suggesting we were merchandise, not human beings. Staying close to Mama and my brothers was my main concern. It was easy to get separated. Mama struggled with the heavy suitcase, finding it difficult to keep up with the flow of people rushing past her. Perhaps one of her migraine headaches was coming on.

We had to pay attention to what was going on around us. Orders of "Go here . . . stand there" **contradicted themselves** until men in civilian clothes wearing white armbands stepped forward to address us, the newcomers.

"You have arrived in Lublin, Poland," one of the men said in **accented German**. "Do not be frightened of us. We are Jews appointed by the SS to keep order and to help get you settled. They call us *Judenrat*. We will now walk to the **ghetto** where you will be housed. Tomorrow you will be assigned work."

Lublin—if I remembered my geography correctly—was in eastern Poland. I was relieved we were going to a ghetto, not a labor camp.

It started to rain, which made walking with a heavy suitcase more difficult. In spite of the rain and fog we found the address given us. It was Novotnastrasse 10, a run-down apartment building surrounded by debris and overgrown weeds. But, oh, what a relief it would be to have a place to stretch out, to wash and sleep!

....

contradicted themselves were confusing

accented German German although he pronounced the words as if he was not from Germany

ghetto poor and dirty neighborhood

Another family already occupied the room assigned us. They were not happy to see us. The woman protested. Mama showed her the paper that had the address and apartment number on it. She made the woman understand **it was not our doing that we were here**. My mother, by now totally exhausted, abandoned her usual pleasant demeanor and reminded the woman that the situation called for sacrifice by all involved.

And so we **settled down** as best we could within the crammed, dark room. Washing or using the one bathroom for the entire floor was **out of the question** for the next hour. Too many people had already lined up.

....

it was not our doing that we were here we were forced to be here

settled down put our things away and rested

out of the question impossible

chapter six

We had **a restless** night. Uncertainty, as well as being unaccustomed to sleeping in a crowded room with strangers, kept us awake.

As soon as it was daylight, we set out for the offices of the *Judenrat* to apply for ration cards and to be assigned a job, for without work there would be no food. The line was already long when we arrived. People filled out forms for job placement and said what **they were most suited for**. I said I had been in training to become a kindergarten teacher before coming here.

"Well, this is your lucky day," the Jewish policeman said. "An SS officer came in yesterday looking for a **nursemaid for** his two young daughters. Working for him means you'll be safe from deportation."

I wanted to ask what he meant by being safe from deportation, but the policeman **waved me on**.

....

a restless an uncomfortable and sleepless
they were most suited for jobs they were good at
nursemaid for woman to help take care of
waved me on told me to continue moving

Close contact with an SS family didn't seem like such a good idea to me; it frightened me. But I was not given a chance to refuse.

Mama was assigned a job in a lamp factory. It would become available in a few days, she was told, as soon as the present holder of the job was transported out. Again there was this talk about deportation and transportation out of the ghetto. Did it mean this was a **temporary place**?

After our ration cards were stamped, we looked for Wolfgang and Selly, who were on the men's side. When there was no sign of them, Mama began to worry.

"The boys are smarter than you think," I assured her. "If they have been taken to work, they will find their way home all by themselves." But inwardly I was just as worried about my brothers as was Mama.

Mama and I decided to explore the ghetto. There would be time enough to go back to the dreary room later. Besides, we needed to **acquaint ourselves with** the place in order to learn how to survive.

Walking up and down cobblestone streets and alleyways, we encountered many people from Germany and Poland. Some were still nicely dressed, looking well fed, while others, dressed in rags, appeared hungry and defeated. The ghetto seemed to be a **paradox between** hope and hopelessness. We passed children carrying books, singing Hebrew songs. The moment I saw them and heard them sing, I felt the **ghetto's spirit** and realized that

....

temporary place place we would leave soon
acquaint ourselves with know about
paradox between place where there was both
ghetto's spirit mood and emotions of the ghetto

in spite of poverty and despair there was a life force here, too.

The winding streets led us to an especially narrow alleyway. There was barely enough room for pedestrians to move, yet an SS man on a horse rode through the center, intimidating people in his way. The stripes on his uniform and the medals pinned to his jacket indicated **a high-ranking** officer. Mama pulled me into a doorway until he passed. Only when he was some distance away did we allow ourselves to breathe.

We walked for hours, and still there was so much more to see, including a bakery where people received bread if they had the required ration cards and the ghetto **marks** to pay for it. Although it wasn't funny, I couldn't help but smile at the fact that the ghetto money looked like the **play** money my brothers and I used in a board game we'd owned. The bread looked wonderful and I would have loved a piece of freshly baked bread, but we didn't dare spend any of our ration cards or the funny money, not knowing how long it had to last.

Then all at once the sun went down. Only moments before, it had been light outside. Mama and I returned to our room feeling cold and hungry, waiting for Wolfgang and Selly to return. Mama listened to every sound coming from the corridor, hoping they would appear any moment. But it wasn't until late that night that my brothers returned, covered with dust and grime. They had been working in a **quarry** loading rocks onto trucks.

"It was grueling," Wolfgang said. "I have never worked so

....

a high-ranking that he was an important
marks money
play fake, pretend
quarry hole where stones are taken from the ground

hard. Our foreman was a Ukrainian with little patience. He beat anyone not working fast enough. It was obvious he hated us."

Our daily visits to the *Judenrat* offices turned into days of wandering through the ghetto as we awaited our job assignments to begin. One morning we came upon a post office and believed it to be just a hoax. Still, I wrote a short note to Papa's sister, Hannah, and her husband, Karl, who had fled to Holland. I never expected the note to reach my uncle and aunt, but weeks later we received a package with rice and beans from them.

We saw people lining up at soup kitchens, trading ration cards for a bowl of soup. Ration cards alone never provided enough food, and people traded clothes and other items they had brought with them for a handful of beets, potatoes, or onions.

I lingered near the ghetto's store at times to check what was available that day. The items were listed on a chalkboard, including the amount of ghetto marks needed to purchase them. **Poles** came into the ghetto to make deals. It was also a place to get news from the outside and **speculate on the duration of our situation**.

One day I saw Erich, the young man I had met on the train, emerge from the store. He told me he had been looking for me to tell me that his father was on the same transport after all. The Nazis beat him up badly at the station in Weimar. **He had not recovered from it.**

"Let me tell you where we live," I said. "If you ever need

....

Poles Polish people

speculate on the duration of our situation talk about how long we would have to live like this

He had not recovered from it. His injuries had not gotten better.

anything, come to us."

After that I didn't see Erich for a long time. The *Judenrat* gave Mama that job in the lamp factory and I was scheduled to start as the nursemaid at the SS man's house.

On the first morning of my new assignment a young police officer from the *Judenrat* accompanied me out of the ghetto to show me the way. His name was Eugen Heiman, and he **was quite talkative**.

"My family and I came with a transport from Stettin a year ago," he said. Because Eugen was a *Judenrat* policeman, he said, he and his family survived quite well.

"As long as you work for an SS family, you and your family will not be deported," he assured me.

"What if I do something to **displease them**?" I asked. "Could they cause trouble for us?" But Eugen seemed to think it would all work out.

"This is it," he said when we arrived at a street lined with **charming villas**. "You are on your own now."

A uniformed maid opened the door. "Wait here," she said, "till I get the mistress."

Moments later the woman of the house, a tall blonde, motioned me to come inside. This is how she greeted me: "How clean are you? Do you wash every day? One never knows with you people."

I was told to hold out my hands **for inspection**. I prided myself on my appearance, and in spite of the difficult

....

was quite talkative talked a lot
displease them make them angry; upset them
charming villas beautiful, large houses
for inspection so that the woman could look at them

58

circumstances I kept myself clean and neat. Satisfied, my employer, Frau Lichter, led me to the children's room, where two little girls awaited me. Eva, the older one, was five and Anneliese four.

"This is Hannelore, one of the Jew girls from the ghetto, like Mindy down in the kitchen," Frau Lichter told them. "She will take care of you."

I didn't know where to look first, at the beautiful **eiderdown quilts encased** in embroidered covers or at the sheer white curtains tied back with sashes. Built-in shelves held dozens and dozens of children's books and toys.

Frau Lichter listed my duties: "Help them bathe, pick out their clothes, take them down to breakfast and lunch, teach them how to read, and keep them amused. You are responsible for them at all times. Is that understood?"

Relying on the skills I had used in the past with my younger cousins, I set out to find the right **tone with which to approach** the two girls. "I know a game," I said. "Would you like to try it? I will start saying a word, then Anneliese will say another, and after that it's Eva's turn. We'll use words to make a sentence, and soon we'll have a story."

The girls thought this was funny. They giggled as the sentences took shape. By the time they were ready to go to the kitchen for breakfast, **I had won them over**.

I **reported for** work every morning except on Sundays, when I was allowed to stay in the ghetto. I grew fond of the two

....

eiderdown quilts encased blankets
tone with which to approach way to talk to
I had won them over the girls liked me
reported for went to

little girls, and they, in turn, adored me. At breakfast and lunch I took them down to the kitchen, where Mindy fed the children and supplied me with plenty of **leftovers** from the day before. How I wished I could take some of this food back to my hungry family! But bringing food into the ghetto was much too risky. I could be sent to a concentration camp for the offense.

We continued to live on Novotnastrasse in the crowded room. If there was any consolation in living in such close quarters with strangers, it was that we got along well with the other family. The woman, like Mama, **was widowed**. But unlike Mama, she still had money to buy food **on the black market**. Uncle Karl and Aunt Hannah had sent another package of rice, beans, and other lentils. It didn't last very long, and soon we began trading whatever clothing we **could spare** for something more to eat.

One day, when I knew there was practically nothing left to trade, I brought home a bag of food from the Lichters' kitchen. "Look, Mama, what I have," I said, proudly displaying some soup bones, three big potatoes, even some leftover roast. "Doesn't this look delicious?"

But Mama was angry. "What if you had been caught? Where would we be then?"

I did not bring home any more food.

Month after month deportations swept through the ghetto. People were often taken away right from work. But I kept clinging to the hope that my job with the Lichters would

....

leftovers food that was not eaten
was widowed had a husband who had died
on the black market through an illegal system
could spare could live without

protect my family and me from deportation. The children had grown attached to me, eagerly awaiting me every morning. As soon as I rang the bell, they would come running to the door to greet me.

All that was to change one afternoon when the *Untersturmführer* came home unexpectedly. I couldn't help but **overhear the heated** conversation that took place.

"I want that girl out of my house now! She has deliberately **alienated the children** from me. All they talk about is Hannelore, Hannelore." Frau Lichter's shrill voice was out of control.

"Are you out of your mind," her husband said, "calling me home in the middle of the day for this nonsense? Are you drunk? Don't think I haven't noticed your drinking."

"So now you, too, are bewitched by the Jew girl!" Frau Lichter shouted.

"You are going too far, Anna," the *Untersturmführer* snapped. "The children are happy with her, and you should be as well. Your servants are Jewish. God knows they have no choice but to serve you well. And the diamonds and jewelry I bring home are taken from Jews, as if you didn't know that already. What is all the fuss about your little nursery maid? Are you jealous of her because the children like her?"

"I demand you throw her out right now. I don't want her near the children," Frau Lichter said.

"She will soon be on one of those transports going to a

....

Untersturmführer girls' father who had an important position in the special German army

overhear the heated listen to the angry

alienated the children kept the children away

concentration camp. I heard from Berlin yesterday. The ghetto is being emptied of all Jews, and we will be going back to our old lifestyle. I'll be out of a job or, worse yet, sent to the Russian front."

Until now I didn't know why the woman disliked me so much, other than that I was Jewish. Now I knew the real truth. **But overshadowing all that was the news of the liquidation of the ghetto.** My heart pounded wildly in my chest. For the rest of the afternoon I walked around in a daze, barely hearing the children's chatter.

The next morning I went back to work as usual. Instead of the children, though, it was Mindy, the cook, who opened the door. "I am sorry, Hannelore," she said. "I was told not to let you in."

I worried about the **impending** liquidation of the ghetto and the danger I had put my family in. I had hoped the *Untersturmführer* would have been able to change his wife's mind, though I was not surprised by the outcome. What was important now was a job—any job—and right away. I hurried to the *Judenrat* office. Erich Neuman, the young man from the train, was there, too. He looked as if he hadn't slept or eaten in days.

"Erich," I said, "you look terrible. What's wrong? Are you being deported?"

He nodded. "Yes, but what my father did to himself is far more upsetting than that. Rather than face another deportation,

....

But overshadowing all that was the news of the liquidation of the ghetto. But more important than that was the news that all of the Jewish people in the ghetto were going to be sent to concentration camps.

impending future, upcoming

he **hanged himself**!"

"Dear God!" Not knowing what to do, I grabbed his hand. "Please, come home with me, if only for a little while. We are sure to have some soup you can eat."

"You tried **playing mother** once before on the train," he said. "No, Hannelore, **it is no use**. I don't think we'll ever meet again."

....

hanged himself killed himself
playing mother taking care of me
it is no use nothing can make me feel better

BEFORE YOU MOVE ON...

1. **Paraphrase** Reread page 55. The author wrote, "The ghetto seemed to be a paradox between hope and hopelessness." What does this mean?

2. **Conclusions** Reread page 61. Why didn't Frau Lichter like Hannelore?

LOOK AHEAD Read pages 64–78 to find out how Eugen tried to help Hannelore.

chapter seven

It sounded like a knock on the door, but I wasn't certain. It was still night; perhaps I had only dreamt of a knock on the door. When it **persisted**, I knew it was real. Mama was already at the door talking to a policeman from the *Judenrat*.

"According to my list, Wolfgang Wolff is here," the man said. "Why don't you make it easy on all of us and get him?"

Mama's words came out **jumbled**: "He did not get a deportation order. You are making a mistake."

"Who said anything about deportation? I am taking him to work. He will be back in the morning."

"You want me to believe that?" Mama shouted.

Desperately grabbing the man's sleeve, she begged him to forget he ever came looking for her son.

"What are you so **excited about**? I told you I would bring him back in the morning. **You have my word.**"

....

persisted did not stop
jumbled unclear
excited about upset for
You have my word. I promise you.

Wolfgang had already dressed. He gave Mama one last **embrace**. She whispered something about God keeping him safe and pressed some bread into his hand. Then he was gone. Mama rocked forward and backward.

"Dear God, why, *why?* What have I done to deserve this?"

I sat near Mama on her bed holding her tight. Both of us shivered in the cold night air, not understanding why Wolfgang was taken from us in the middle of the night when he was still able to work.

I promised Mama that as soon as it was daylight and I was allowed on the street, I would go to the *Judenrat*. A young policeman I knew might be able to help get Wolfgang back, I told her. For the rest of the night we comforted each other with **false hope**.

At the first sign of daylight I went looking for Eugen Heiman, the young man who had escorted me on the first day of my job at the Lichters. I had seen him several times on the street. He always **flirted**, but I was too shy to respond. Eugen was surprised to see me so early in the morning.

"What brings you here at this hour?" he asked.

I told him what had happened and that the policeman had assured my mother Wolfgang would be back in the morning. I wanted him released right now and hoped Eugen could help.

"What makes you think I can do anything like that?" He pushed his policeman's cap to the back of his head and looked at me with **a measure of arrogance**.

....

embrace hug
false hope talk that we could save Wolfgang
flirted acted like he liked me
a measure of arrogance pride

"You probably know where he is. Please, help us get him back. He is only a boy!"

Eugen was blunt: "You are too late. Your brother left hours ago for Majdanek. I suppose you know what that means?"

"Majdanek!" I cried out. "Oh my God, what will I tell Mama?"

"He didn't have to go if you would have paid attention to me. A girl as pretty as you should **take advantage of her looks**. You kept ignoring me every time I came near you. I might have been able to save your brother."

"Stop it! Can't you see what this is doing to me?" I turned to leave.

"Think about what I said," he shouted after me. "Your younger brother doesn't have to **wind up like that** if you decide to be nice to me."

I ran out of the office in disgust. *You swine,* I thought. *How dare you talk to me that way! I am only seventeen, and you want me to be a bad girl and fool around with you. Never!*

I ran back to the room to tell Mama that I had talked to the policeman. I was vague, assuring her my policeman friend would do anything that could be done. She knew right away that I wasn't telling the truth.

"I would like to believe you, Hannelore, but can I?"

Mama cried herself to sleep every night. A mother knows when her children are in danger.

....

take advantage of her looks use her beauty to get what she wants or needs

wind up like that be taken away

★ ★ ★

My new job, working in a factory making parts for heavy vehicles used by the German Wehrmacht, was not all that bad. One afternoon while I was on my way home, I saw Eugen coming toward me. Trying to avoid **a confrontation with him, I quickly mingled** with all the other workers, but he followed me anyway.

"I would like to walk you home," he said.

I kept on walking as if he didn't exist.

"I can't blame you for ignoring me," he persisted. "I behaved badly the morning you came to me for help. Please, forgive me."

"Try not to insult me again and I'll forgive you," I answered.

"I want to help you and your family."

"Help us? What is it you propose to do for us?"

"The ghetto will be liquidated any day now. Unless you go **into hiding**, you'll be in big trouble."

"We have no money, **no connections**. I wouldn't know where to hide."

"That is where I come in," Eugen said. "I know of such places."

He told me that he had been thinking about me ever since the morning I ran out of his office and how he should have known I wasn't that kind of girl. "Talk it over with your mother and let me know soon," he said.

....

a confrontation with him, I quickly mingled an argument with him, I quickly walked and talked

into hiding to a place and hide from the Nazis

no connections we do not know anyone who can help us

"**No strings attached?**" I asked before we parted. "You want nothing in return?"

"You have my word of honor."

Mama greeted me in the hallway. She had been anxiously waiting for me. "Why are you late? Don't you know how I worry when you and Selly don't come home on time?"

I explained about the liquidation of the ghetto and Eugen's offer. "He also told me he would put each of us in a different hiding place. Can you accept that, Mama?"

"Do I have a choice?"

Our last night on Novotnastrasse was an emotional one. We **huddled together, reminiscing** about times past, talking about Papa and Wolfgang.

I remember Mama holding a prayer book in her hand, reading **psalms**. Her tears covered the pages. I could barely hold back my own tears, wondering if we would see one another again.

At the first sign of light we closed the door at Novotnastrasse 10, leaving our remaining possessions behind. Each went in a different direction. It was October 1942.

....

No strings attached? I do not have to do anything for you?

huddled together, reminiscing sat close to each other, thinking

psalms stories and songs from the prayer book

chapter eight

Crawling through the narrow entrance of the tunnel wasn't easy, but I managed it without bumping my head. Suddenly a man shining a flashlight into my face stopped me.

"It's all right, you can let her in," I heard Eugen say. "Mordechai **saw to it** that no one followed her."

Eugen had given me instructions on how to reach this hiding place. Getting here had been **like an obstacle course**. First I had to enter a house on Halinastrasse, making sure I wasn't followed. The tunnel's entrance was in the cellar of that house. After removing several cleverly concealed planks, I lowered myself onto a narrow underground walkway, careful of every step. When I reached the end, I found myself near a garden fence. There I was met by a man who led me to the real tunnel. The precautions were necessary, Eugen explained, because of the many **would-be informers walking around**.

....

saw to it made sure

like an obstacle course very difficult

would-be informers walking around people walking around who might tell the police about the tunnel

While Eugen was busy directing other people into the tunnel, I was left **to my own devices**. It was extremely dark. More and more people came. I couldn't see them, but I felt their presence. The silence was broken only by an occasional whisper.

Hours passed. Eugen came once, shining a dim flashlight in my direction. He handed me a chocolate bar. It only took two bites to finish it. I had not tasted chocolate since I left home.

There was nothing to do but wait. From above came screams and cries and shots being fired. Dogs barked, adding to our fear that we might be discovered. I recited all the Hebrew prayers I **knew by heart**.

Hours later the noises stopped. We waited a long time before opening the entrance, fearing the silence might be a trick to get us out. A brisk wind whirled through streets **dancing with discarded scarves** and other articles left behind. Otherwise the ghetto was deserted.

I immediately looked for Eugen, hoping to learn where he had hidden Mama and Selly. When I couldn't find him, I set out on my own, looking into doorways and courtyards, going from house to house. I became lost in the inner ghetto, where one little street wound around another.

Over and over I softly called their names, but there was no response. A man in a dark overcoat seemed to be following me. I fled, remembering Eugen's warning about informants.

When **evening drew nearer**, I sat down on the stoop of a house. My hopes shattered, I sobbed into my hands. When I

....

to my own devices alone
knew by heart could remember; had memorized
dancing with discarded scarves filled with clothes
evening drew nearer it was almost evening

looked up, I saw Eugen, **grim-faced**, running toward me.

"I've looked for you for almost an hour. You must hurry. The Germans are back. Their trucks are waiting to take us away!"

"What about my mother and brother? I can't leave without them!"

"You can see they are not here. **Chances are** they were discovered. I did my best, you have to believe that. Come with me now. They'll shoot you if you **disobey**."

....

grim-faced looking upset; looking worried
Chances are I believe
disobey do not do what they tell you to do

chapter nine

"Faster, faster, you pig," an SS man yelled, **hurling** me onto a truck already filled with many people. There was barely enough room to stand. Fortunately, the ride was short.

The same words were repeated when the truck halted. I got out as quickly as I could to avoid being hit. There was only one thing on my mind: finding Mama and Selly.

The camp was surrounded by a **barbed-wire fence**. Inside the camp's main square was the so-called Appellplatz, the place to be counted and humiliated and, as I found out later, where prisoners were punished. Lining the square were barracks. The overseer, a prisoner herself, of the barrack to which I was assigned stood at the entrance of the building. She looked like a farm girl. Her sturdiness and rosy complexion **belied the fact that she was a camp inmate**.

"Here you do as I tell you," she addressed us newcomers.

....

hurling pushing
barbed-wire fence fence with wires attached to it
belied the fact that she was a camp inmate made her look like she was not a prisoner

"When I blow the whistle, you will run."

It was obvious not only to me but to many of the women that had it not been for the **nightmarish turn of events**, this girl would never have risen to a position of power. After issuing us a thin blanket and a tin cup, she disappeared behind a **curtained-off cubicle**.

I waited eagerly for the evening meal, having had nothing to eat all day. When the food arrived, I was among the first to stand in line for the brown water that was supposedly coffee and a slice of bread with beet jam. It did little to satisfy my hunger.

Suddenly I was aware of a woman staring at me. "Forgive me," she said. "For a moment I thought you were my daughter. You look so much like her. We were separated a few weeks ago, and with every new transport that arrives my hopes of finding her go up."

"I know the feeling," I said. "Until this morning my mother, my younger brother, and I lived together in the ghetto. We lost one another during the liquidation. I hope they are here. Does this place have a name?"

"This is Belzyce," the woman said. "It is not bad, as labor camps go." She invited me to **bunk** near her, where the straw was still fresh.

When Eugen came looking for me the next day, I asked for news about Mama and Selly. He had nothing to report. For him the good news was that he was again a *Judenrat* policeman. And he had **the prospect of** a job for me.

....

nightmarish turn of events terrible situation
curtained-off cubicle curtain in front of her room
bunk sleep on a bed
the prospect of found

"There is a very small **infirmary** here. They need a nurse."

I reminded him that I was not trained as a nurse.

"You don't need nursing skills to work in a camp infirmary. I know the doctor who runs the place. We came from the same town. He will **take you on** as a favor to me."

When it was settled, I started work in the infirmary. The small wooden barrack located at the end of the compound held only six beds. A cheerful redheaded man dressed in a white coat looked at me through thick lenses.

"Janek is the name," he said, taking a bow. "About time they sent me a helper. Patients come and go. No one wants to stay. You see, it's not healthy staying too long." He laughed, assuming I knew what he meant.

I appreciated his **grim sense of humor**, his easy manner, and looked forward to working with him. In one corner stood a cast-iron stove. I assumed it was there to boil water for sterilizing instruments, but I saw other possibilities. With a little bit of luck I might beg a potato or turnip from the kitchen. My tin cup would serve as a pot.

Dr. Mosbach, a tall, broad-shouldered man in a white coat, soon arrived. He greeted me warmly and told me I would be safe here. We had only one patient that day, and after examining him, the doctor left.

It was still dark when I awoke the next morning, but I could tell by the sky that **daybreak was at hand**. I dressed quickly, grateful to have my loden cloth coat and two sweaters to keep

....

infirmary hospital
take you on let you work there
grim sense of humor ability to make jokes
daybreak was at hand it would soon be morning

me warm. It was all I had left. Crossing the dimly lit camp, I walked briskly to the infirmary. Janek was already there.

"You are early," he greeted me.

"Hunger kept me awake," I said.

"Help yourself to hot water," he said. "It's on the stove."

I placed my hands around the tin cup, almost burning myself. But it felt good, and I pretended I was sipping hot cocoa.

The whistle blew, barrack doors opened, and people ran to the place of assembly. Working in the infirmary **exempted me from reporting** there. Later Janek went to the camp kitchen to pick up our ration of "coffee" and a slice of bread with a pat of margarine.

In the afternoon a patient arrived. I tried to **engage him in conversation**, but all I got out of him was, "When will the doctor be here?"

"How did you get that bullet in your leg? Where did you come from?" Dr. Mosbach fired question after question and let the patient know he would not touch him before he told him everything. Reluctant at first, the patient soon told his story **in a rush of words**.

"I had been hiding with a Polish farmer for over a year. I paid him well, but he wanted more and more money. He already had everything I owned, and I had nothing more to give him. Yesterday he tried to **chase me off** his property. When I refused to leave, he shot me."

Dr. Mosbach went to work immediately. The patient was

....

exempted me from reporting meant that I did not have to go
engage him in conversation talk to him
in a rush of words completely, quickly
chase me off force me to leave

in great pain, there was no **anesthetic**, and the instruments were old.

When I returned the next morning, the patient was gone.

My own life started to get better than it had been in a long time. Janek had a friend who worked in the kitchen and supplied us with an occasional potato or turnip, which we roasted on the stove. Even the soup portions were bigger because of his friend. But food was not my greatest concern. I was more concerned with knowing where my family was and how they were coping.

I liked looking out the window, especially at sunset. The amber sky often **moved me to tears**. When the sunset was beautiful, I was even more vulnerable, wondering if Mama and the boys were able to see what I saw.

I had worked in the infirmary for just over a month when Janek told me to get a bed ready, preferably the one in the far corner near the stove.

"Why that one?" I asked.

"One of the *Kapos* **went to work on** a young boy. I heard he is **in bad shape**. He'll need to be kept warm."

I'd barely gotten the hot water and bandages ready when the door opened and the patient was brought in on a stretcher. His clothes were in tatters, and he was covered with blood. The minute they tossed him onto the bed and I saw his face, I screamed.

....

anesthetic medicine to help the man feel less pain
moved me to tears made me cry
went to work on badly beat
in bad shape really hurt; not doing well

76

"What is it?" Janek asked.

"This is my brother. It's Selly!" I cried.

I became hysterical, screaming and running in circles. Janek grabbed me by the shoulders and demanded I **get hold of myself**. He went over to the bed.

"Can you hear me, Selly? Your sister, Hannelore, is right beside you. You're safe now."

We sponged my brother's bruised face, removed his tattered clothes, and wet his swollen lips. Blood had **congealed** around his eyes and mouth. Selly wailed and moaned. If he recognized me, he didn't show it.

Dr. Mosbach came immediately and probed him all over. Selly winced and cried at the slightest touch. It was agonizing to watch.

"Our main problem is a **collapsed** lung," Dr. Mosbach told me. "The broken ribs and bruises will heal in time. It's the lung that concerns me. It may never fully function again. We'll keep him here for a few days, then we have to let him disappear in one of the barracks. He will not be able to work for quite a while, if at all."

I knew we had to get Selly out of the infirmary fast. Leaving a patient there more than a few days would mean **a death sentence**.

Janek came with a bowl of soup. After I fed my brother, carefully spooning the soup into his mouth so as not to touch the bruised lips, he was able to talk in halting sentences. A *Kapo*

....

get hold of myself calm down
congealed dried up
collapsed badly damaged
a death sentence that he would be killed

in a foul mood had picked him **at random** for a beating. With no one to stop him the *Kapo* kept on beating him until he tired.

I would have liked to stay by Selly's side during the night, but I couldn't risk it. It was against camp rules. When I returned early the next morning, Selly was awake. I brought all the food I had saved up, but it wasn't enough to fill him. He was not only in pain, he was also terribly hungry.

Although his rib cage was bandaged and he was far from well, he had to leave the infirmary. Dr. Mosbach arranged for him to do **light chores** in one of the barracks. I saw him daily. He was not getting much better, but there was nothing to be done under the circumstances. We talked about our hiding places in the ghetto and the fact that Selly had been here in this camp the entire time without me knowing it.

"Did you see where they took Mama? Did they discover her hiding place?"

Selly didn't have a single answer to my many questions.

....

at random without reason
light chores easy work

BEFORE YOU MOVE ON...

1. **Inference** Eugen was able to help Hannelore. Why was he in a better position than most Jewish people?

2. **Conclusions** Reread pages 74–75. How was Hannelore's situation in Belzyce better than most?

LOOK AHEAD Read pages 79–92 to learn about a camp called "paradise."

chapter ten

The thought of spending the rest of the war in Belzyce was strangely comforting to me, and in my mind it was entirely possible. Here in Belzyce I could look after Selly, **to a certain extent**, and after the war I would seek out the best medical treatment for him. Perhaps a good doctor could restore full function to his lungs.

Eugen remained a good friend. He came to the infirmary often while **making his rounds of** the camp.

But just when everything seemed to be going well, there was disturbing news. **Rumors went around** that Belzyce was being liquidated. Eugen confirmed the rumors. We would all be sent to Budzyn, a nearby camp that had a commandant who was said to be not only ruthless but also crazy. Shooting prisoners for no reason at all was a daily exercise for him.

My first thought was of Selly and what would happen to

....

to a certain extent as much as I could
making his rounds of doing his work around
Rumors went around People started to say

him. Obviously, he was not well. Always fatigued, he never had enough to eat, and hard work was much too taxing for a boy with a collapsed lung.

My days were occupied with caring for patients and cleaning the infirmary, so for the time being I **dismissed the thought of** the camp's liquidation. Weeks later a group of Nazis, accompanied by a man wearing a white armband that identified him as a member of a *Judenrat*, came into camp. They spent hours in the office going through files. From time to time food and liquor was brought in and **snatches of their conversation were circulated** to us, the anxious inmates. The Nazis had come from a nearby camp called Krašnik to select craftsmen, tailors, and shoemakers to take with them before Belzyce was closed.

When I saw the Nazis walking toward the infirmary, I was suddenly struck with unexplained terror. I retreated into the corner, behind the cast-iron stove, as though I could make myself invisible.

Soon the door opened. The tallest of the SS men entered first. His uniform was decorated with medals. "The camp infirmary, **Herr** Commandant," the man from the *Judenrat* explained. "Very efficient; it meets all the camp's needs."

But the commandant paid little attention. His gaze was directed at me, behind the stove.

"Are you hiding from me?" he asked cheerfully. His speech was slurred, as if he'd had too much to drink.

....

dismissed the thought of did not think about

snatches of their conversation were circulated some of the things they talked about were told

Herr Mister (in German)

I avoided looking at him. That made him roar with laughter.

"She is pretty, but can she talk?"

"Herr Commandant," one of his men said, "we've just been told the girl is retarded."

"Nonsense. She is not retarded. She is afraid of me. We'll take her with us to Krašnik. We need a nurse."

There was some whispering; then the man from the *Judenrat* stepped forward.

"The girl is not a nurse, Herr Commandant."

"Do not contradict me. I said she was coming with us. Pack her up!"

No longer interested in the infirmary, the SS men departed, leaving the man from the *Judenrat* behind.

"You'd better get yourself ready right away. We'll be leaving shortly," he said to me. I was still crouched behind the stove.

"I cannot leave," I said. "I have a younger brother in this camp. He is not well. He needs me!"

"Whether your brother needs you or not is unimportant. The commandant asked for you, and we'd better do as he says. **Considering the state he was in**, he may not remember you by the time we get back to Krašnik, but I can't take that chance."

"Hannelore, do as he tells you." Janek's voice seemed far away. "You are the lucky one. The rest of us are going to Budzyn, where Untersturmführer Feix **reigns**."

"Don't you see, Janek? I can't go!" I cried. "How is Selly to survive on his own? And did you see the way that drunkard

....

Considering the state he was in Because he was drunk
reigns rules

looked at me?"

"You may not know it, Hannelore, but Krašnik is a paradise. You'll see when you get there. I wish I could go."

"I don't care about this paradise if I can't take Selly along. And what if the Nazi remembers me? What then?"

The man from the *Judenrat* grew impatient. "**It will be my neck** if you are not in Krašnik, so stop arguing and forget the idea of taking your brother along."

I ran across the camp looking for Selly. Sometimes he would be near the kitchen, hoping to catch some potato peelings or anything else that **was edible**. Today he was not there, nor was he in his barrack. After gathering my few possessions, I went to say good-bye to the woman who had befriended me, then hurried back to the infirmary to leave a note with Janek.

Please explain to Selly what happened, I wrote. *And, Janek, he needs help!*

We went by military truck. There were only four other inmates from Belzyce and the man from the *Judenrat.* One SS guard drove, while the other rode behind us in the back. I was terrified the entire trip by the thought of the drunken commandant and what he might have planned for me.

By the time the truck stopped, night had fallen. An SS guard opened the gate to a dimly lit compound. There were no barracks here, only private houses. A wire fence surrounded the houses, but aside from that, one would not have known this

....

It will be my neck I will be punished
was edible could be eaten

was a camp holding Jewish prisoners. **Janek's words came to mind**: "Krašnik is a paradise."

The driver called to a Jewish policeman patrolling the grounds: "Avraham, go wake my daughter. Tell her I need a bed for the night for this girl. You find a place for the men."

A short time later the policeman came back. "Your daughter was not very happy having her sleep disturbed, Manek."

Manek mumbled something while leading me into a house. We walked through a long corridor, stopping at the end.

"You can stay here for the night."

There was a full moon. Its reflection **cast a glow over** the lace curtains covering the windows. I had not seen such a beautiful sight in a very long time. *My God,* I thought, *how is it possible that Jews still live like this? Perhaps this is paradise.*

Out of habit I placed my meager belongings under my head as I prepared to lie down on the soft couch, **a long-forgotten luxury**. At last I fell asleep dreaming of Mama in her Shabbat dress.

When the first rays of sunshine filtered through the curtains, I rose. I saw women dressed in oversized shawls walking toward the gate, returning a short time later with pitchers of milk. What kind of world had I stumbled into, I wondered, where Jews drink milk and live in houses?

"I have brought you breakfast," a woman entering the room said. She was rather plump and looked well cared for. Aware of the shabbiness of my own clothes, I felt embarrassed. In Belzyce

....

Janek's words came to mind I remembered what Janek said before I left

cast a glow over shined on

a long-forgotten luxury something that I had not been able to enjoy in a long time

I had looked like a beggar, as did all the inmates. Here I stood out like one.

I **marveled at the delicacies** put before me. There was real coffee and slices of bread with white cheese. Later in the day Manek explained to me that my presence here had created a problem.

"Frankly, I don't quite know what to do with you. I have called the *Judenrat* together; perhaps they have a solution."

Eyeing me with suspicion, members of the *Judenrat* questioned Manek. "Did you at least try talking him out of bringing her here?"

"Do you have to ask? Of course I tried, but you know him when he is drunk and sees a pretty face. If we are lucky, he will have forgotten about her already. However, I couldn't take the chance of leaving her behind. What if he *does* remember her?"

"You **mishandled the** situation!" Angry shouts filled the room. "She is your responsibility. *You* take care of her."

From the first day on I was made to feel like an unwelcome intruder. I was excluded from gatherings, **shunned** by the other inmates. The commandant, however, didn't ask for me. I was quite sure he didn't remember me at all, and that was lucky.

Aside from being lonely, the calm and relative peace that existed in Krašnik was a welcome change. In Belzyce people had to beg for food, but everyone here was well fed. I was given food and a room of my own in one of the houses in exchange for cleaning and washing clothes.

....

marveled at the delicacies was amazed by the food

Eyeing Looking at

mishandled the made a mistake in this

shunned ignored

Manek, who was obviously the head of the *Judenrat* here, took me aside and told me that I would be working in the front office at the camp's **reception desk**.

"Since you speak flawless German, this is a perfect place for you. I must warn you, however. Do not **probe into our affairs**, ever. This is a warning. You are a guest here, but that can change at any time."

Since I didn't know how the camp operated and why it was so comfortable here—why everyone had a decent house, enough food, and why there were few SS men around—I didn't know what to think. This was no ordinary labor camp.

My work began the same day. It was easy, and I was glad to have something to do. When the phone rang, I answered it in German. Almost everyone asked to speak to Manek. He assured them in his halting German, mixed with Yiddish, that it was all right to make an appointment through the new receptionist. She was completely trustworthy. The callers usually identified themselves by rank. There was a Captain Schlesinger, a Colonel Weiler from the Waffen-SS, even several Polish officials. The question they **posed** was always the same: "**Fräulein**, are you sure no one else is coming this afternoon?"

I was at my desk every morning making appointments, greeting people. But there wasn't enough work to keep me busy. Sometimes other inmates dropped by the office. They began to trust me more and more and started talking to me. A Jewish dentist used a room above the reception area as an office.

....

reception desk desk where guests were welcomed
probe into our affairs ask about what we are doing
posed asked
Fräulein Miss (in German)

He treated patients from within the camp as well as outsiders, SS people, and Poles. When he wasn't busy, he'd drop by my desk **making small talk**. One day I questioned him about Krašnik, about how this place worked. He walked away without answering, and I didn't see him again for many weeks. Everyone I talked to **was evasive**. Finally I understood: They were afraid I might betray them. And I had nothing to contribute to a camp where, evidently, everyone had to pay to remain there.

Captain Schlesinger was one of the visitors who came to the camp on a weekly basis. He stopped at my desk now and then. We talked about the weather and how I liked Poland—as if he didn't know I was not here of my own free will. From the very beginning I was puzzled **over the resemblance he bore to** a Jewish boy I had known in Berlin. His name too was Schlesinger. I **became obsessed with the idea** that the captain might be a Jew in disguise. I so wanted this to be true that I created a fantasy around him. I saw him as someone living with a false identity, someone who had come to rescue Jews.

One day Captain Schlesinger stayed longer than usual. After some meaningless talk he became more personal. "Judging from your dialect, you come from northern Germany," he said.

"Yes, I do." I realized that I had been too quick to answer. "I lived in Aurich, Ostfriesland, not far from the North Sea."

"That makes us practically neighbors," he joked. "I come from Hamburg. Have you ever been there?"

"Yes, many times. My mother's cousin lives there. He owns

....

making small talk to talk to me about unimportant things
was evasive would not answer my questions
over the resemblance he bore to because he looked like
became obsessed with the idea could not stop thinking

a haberdashery store."

"It wouldn't be Salo Walden's haberdashery, would it?"

"Uh, yes," I muttered. "What a coincidence."

Schlesinger, appearing somewhat embarrassed, scratched his head. "The last time I saw Salo was a year ago. He and his family were on their way to Riga . . . deported, just like yourself. I personally sealed the apartment."

I didn't know what to say. **My heart skipped a few beats** when I heard the word *deported*. I hoped they were still alive.

"I bought hats and ties from Salo Walden before all this happened," Schlesinger continued. "Too bad he is a Jew, or I'd still be buying from him."

Unable to sleep that night, I thought of nothing else but Captain Schlesinger. It was impossible to **figure him out**. One moment I believed him to be a Jew in disguise, the next moment I didn't trust him. It was all so confusing.

When I didn't see him for several weeks, I thought he had been **transferred**, and in a way I was glad for that. But he did come back one day, leaning over my desk and laughing.

"I see our little Jewish girl is still here. I was wondering if they had sent *you* to Riga yet. Sooner or later you'll all go."

He went into Manek's office and I thought I had seen the last of him, but on the way out he stopped at my desk again. I was totally unprepared for what he had to say next: "I can get you out of here."

I thought I hadn't heard right.

....

My heart skipped a few beats I was nervous
figure him out understand him
transferred sent to another place to work

"I can get you papers, **Aryan papers**," he continued. "I let a Polish girl disappear this week. You can have her apartment, her clothes. She was about your size. It's certainly better than going to Riga. No one comes back from Riga, and how long do you think Krašnik can last? Think it over."

I didn't know what to say. Perhaps my first **perception of** him had been correct—that he was a Jew and wanted to save fellow Jews. My decision to accept or decline his offer changed from hour to hour. In the end I convinced myself that he was trying to help me survive and that perhaps he knew something was about to happen in Krašnik.

The next time he came into the office, I was ready.

"You'll have to get a pass from Manek that allows you to leave the camp," he told me. "How about next Thursday? Tell him you have to help me with some office work."

It sounded innocent enough, so I asked Manek for the pass. "Are you sure about this?" he asked.

The look on his face was one of reluctance. But the moment passed, and I said, yes, I wanted the pass.

On Thursday, Captain Schlesinger arrived. I followed him out the gate and through the streets of Krašnik, feeling **apprehensive** but excited. Not having been on an ordinary street since leaving Weimar, I stared at everything around me. Life seemed to be normal . . . for non-Jewish people. Girls in high heels walked the streets, as did women with shopping bags and children carrying satchels on their way home from school.

....

Aryan papers papers that show you are not Jewish

perception of thought about

The look on his face was one of reluctance. It seemed like he did not want to give me a pass.

apprehensive worried, nervous

When I slowed down a little to take all this in, the captain told me to hurry. It wasn't what he said but how he said it that gave me a fright. His voice was harsh, and I immediately sensed a change in him. *Oh God,* I silently prayed, *let this turn out all right. I am no longer sure if he is out to save me or to kill me.*

After we had walked a while in total silence, he ordered me into a building. My suspicion that something bad was about to happen grew when he started pushing me up the stairs to the third floor.

The apartment we entered was **in total disarray**. The floor was littered with the contents of drawers and cupboards and two pictures of a pretty girl in a summer dress. The pictures had been trampled on. I remembered what he had told me about "letting" a Polish girl disappear. Was he going to do the same thing to me? How could I have **been so blind, not seeing through his scheme**?

He did not keep me guessing very long as to why he had brought me here. Grabbing me by my hair, he said, "Whore, before I am finished with you, you'll tell me about the commandant. I'll fix that swine for getting involved with a Jewish pig!"

"What are you talking about?" I began. But then it suddenly became clear why I was here. He never had any intention of helping me. All he wanted to do was **bring the commandant down**.

He yanked my hair again. "Tell me now or I'll have to

....

in total disarray very messy

been so blind, not seeing through his scheme not known that he was trying to trick me

bring the commandant down get the leader of the camp out of power

kill you."

"I—I have never even talked to the c-commandant," I stuttered, too dazed to speak clearly.

"He brought you to Krašnik!"

"Yes, he did, but since then I have had no contact with him. He forgot about me."

"You are lying, you filthy, dirty slut!" He squeezed my arm too tight.

"You're hurting me!" I cried out.

Abruptly, he started to laugh. It sounded unnatural, almost **maniacal**. I was frantic. Before I knew it, he had **pinned** my arms behind my back. Then he threw me down on the bed.

"Are you ready to tell me now?"

"There is *nothing* to tell. Please, let me go!" I begged.

He threw himself on me, ripping my clothes off. His gun and the buckle of his belt pressed into my belly. I heard a zipper being undone and pleaded for him to stop. He breathed heavily and smelled like an animal **in heat**, paying no attention to my cries. I tried sliding away, but each time he yanked me by my hair, pulling me under him again. With my arms still pinned behind me he did what he set out to do and finished by punching me in the face. At that moment the phone rang.

"All right, all right," I heard him say to the caller in an agitated voice. "I'll be there in fifteen minutes."

I got up, arranging my torn clothes as best I could.

"I will come back to kill you if you talk to anyone about

....

maniacal crazy, insane

pinned pushed

in heat ready to reproduce; trying to breed

this," he said in a **menacing voice**. "Now get out."

He pushed me back down the stairs, into the streets. I was bleeding profusely and my legs could barely carry me, but he rushed me to the camp's entrance and left me at the gate.

If I had hoped to get to my room unseen. I was mistaken. Manek was waiting for me, visibly agitated.

"Look at you! He beat you up **in spite of what you told him**. Did you think you could save yourself by **selling us out**?"

"Why . . . why didn't you warn me if you knew what he was after?" I cried.

"You'll have to figure that out for yourself. I'd like to know one thing: What did you tell him?"

"Nothing! I had nothing to tell him. I don't know what goes on here. He thought I had something going on with the commandant."

I left him there and hurried to my room, where I relived the horror of the last few hours and tried to stop the bleeding. Avraham, the *Judenrat* policeman, soon called for me.

"Go away!" I shouted.

"You are wanted at the front office. You'd better come with me."

I obeyed, fearful of being hurt again. When we reached the office, Avraham told me to wait. From beyond the closed door came loud voices.

"You should have stopped me from bringing her here. You are responsible!" The commandant's words were angry.

....

menacing voice way that scared me

in spite of what you told him even after you told him what he wanted to know

selling us out telling him what we are doing

"She couldn't tell him anything. She knows absolutely nothing," Manek responded. "Herr Commandant, **we have nothing to fear from her**."

"I want you to get rid of her, *now*."

"Herr Commandant," Manek pleaded, "I have a better idea. Let me take her to Budzyn. Untersturmführer Feix will know what to do with her, and **our hands will remain clean**."

I **passed out cold** and never heard how it ended.

....

we have nothing to fear from her she cannot get us into trouble

our hands will remain clean no one will know that we were involved

passed out cold fainted; became unconscious

BEFORE YOU MOVE ON...

1. **Comparisons** Reread pages 82–84. How was camp Krašnik different from Belzyce?

2. **Assumption** What did Hannelore assume about Captain Schlesinger that got her into trouble?

LOOK AHEAD Read pages 93–107 to learn more about how Jewish people were mistreated.

chapter eleven

Manek and I had not spoken one word since we boarded the same military truck that had brought me to Krašnik some months earlier. Finally, before leaving me at the entrance to the Budzyn camp, Manek said, "I saved your life by bringing you here."

"It's because of you that I am in this **predicament**," I snapped. "You should have warned me about that **madman**. Do you understand what he has done to me? *Do you?*"

"I couldn't take the chance. You might have told him things. What did he promise you?"

"My freedom, false papers, going to Germany as a foreign worker. I believed him. How was I to know what he was after? What could I have told him? I was **kept in the dark** the entire time."

Budzyn looked like an army compound at first, but the

....

predicament bad situation
madman crazy man
kept in the dark not given any information

barbed wire and **searchlights overhead told another story**.

Quite unexpectedly, my eyes focused on a man standing only a few feet away. He was dressed in a Polish army uniform, complete with a three-cornered hat that could barely contain the chestnut-colored hair sticking out from under it. His uniform identified him as a prisoner of war. A patch sewn to his uniform showed he was Jew.

Our eyes met only for a second, long enough for me to notice how beautiful—and sad—his were. The moment was interrupted by the shrill voice of an SS woman.

"You there," she said, pointing at me. "Go to the shower, you filthy slut."

The shower was big enough for a hundred people, but I was the only one there now.

"So, where did they find you?" The attendant tried being humorous. He turned the shower on. I felt relieved to wash away the foul odor of Captain Schlesinger even though the water was cold and made me shiver.

I dressed quickly under the watchful eye of the attendant, who handed me a bundle of clothes. My own had already been taken away. Luckily, I had hidden the photos of my family under a loose plank in the bench. Without the attendant noticing it, I slipped the photos in my shoe.

Wondering what to do next, I walked back to the camp's entrance. The man with the beautiful eyes was still there. This time I looked away, ashamed of what had happened to me.

....

searchlights overhead told another story the bright lights
at the top of the buildings showed that it was a
concentration camp

Our eyes met We looked at each other

My hair hung in wet strings around my face; my dress was even shabbier than the one I had brought from Krašnik.

The same SS woman who had ordered me to the shower was waiting. "Let's go," she snapped as she escorted me inside one of the barracks. "Regina, this one is **all yours**. Watch her closely."

Regina introduced herself as the *Blockälteste,* the one responsible for this barrack. She, too, was an inmate here.

As it was early morning, a loud whistle called everyone to the place of assembly. Shaking the straw off their clothing, the women from my barrack filed into the square. I followed them there. All of us were packed tightly together. I **was repulsed by** the odor of their unwashed bodies. I didn't know yet why they smelled or why their clothing was stained. I would learn only later that one dress, worn day and night, and only an occasional shower produced that odor.

Regina was not unkind. She **hurried us on**, saying, "It's for your own good to be on time." Her Yiddish was understandable to me; her Polish was not.

Back in the barrack a young girl approached me. "I haven't seen you here before. When did you arrive?"

I explained that I had come during the night.

"There is room on my bunk," the girl said. "Up here, on the third level."

And so it was that I instantly became friends with the girl named Fella, who not only was beautiful to look at but cheerful **in spite of our** surroundings.

....

all yours staying in your barrack
was repulsed by felt sick because of
hurried us on told us to walk quickly
in spite of our even though we were living in terrible

"How do you manage to act as if this is a normal place?" I wanted to know.

"I pretend it *is* normal," Fella answered, flashing her almond-shaped eyes.

Having a friend **made all the difference**. Now I had someone to talk to, to share my fears and hopes with. Fella was practical as well. She offered a lot of good advice. When I ate my portion of bread too fast, Fella showed me how to make it last longer by taking very small bites.

"Sometimes they withhold the noon soup as a form of punishment. It's hard to deal with that when you are so hungry, but you will get used to it," she assured me.

It was incredible what had happened to me within a span of twenty-four hours. First I had been violated and had been close to losing my life. Now I had found a wonderful friend who would help me cope with the hardships of this camp.

But my first day in Budzyn had just begun, and it would stretch into a very long and painful experience. The backbreaking work of lifting rocks onto trucks for road building, **coupled with** the fact that I had been up all night with only a slice of bread for breakfast, made me sluggish. I became exhausted in a matter of hours and **fell behind in** my work.

Fella kept a watchful eye on me. "The overseer, the *Kapo*, has been looking your way for some time now. You must work faster, Hannelore, or he will punish you. He is mean."

My back felt as if it was breaking and I **grew lightheaded**,

....

made all the difference made my life better
coupled with and
fell behind in was not able to do all of
grew lightheaded felt like I would faint; felt dizzy

yet I continued to work as if my life depended on it—which indeed it did.

At noon we were given time to sit on the ground and eat the soup that was brought to us in large cauldrons. Even the odd smell of the **watery soup didn't dampen my appetite**, and I held out my cup in eager anticipation of my portion.

All too soon the whistle blew, calling us back to work. The blisters on my hands had opened, making it even more painful to hold the shovel. Fella's promise that the afternoon hours would be better because a different *Kapo,* more humane than the first one, would be guarding us was small comfort.

The afternoon dragged on. It seemed as if it would never end. The sun had already gone down, and we were still at work. Fatigued, I asked Fella to tell me how much longer we would have to work before they returned us to camp.

"It's almost dark now," she said. "They always return us to camp before it gets dark."

Her assurances that the first days in this camp were the hardest, that I would soon get used to the routine, did little to **ease my weariness**. The march back to camp was **uneventful**, but our day was not over yet. As we'd done in the morning, we again had to stand at the assembly place and be counted. Untersturmführer Feix, our camp commandant, was in no hurry. Seeing us looking tired and hungry seemed to amuse him. This evening he played his favorite game with the male prisoners. The command "Caps off, caps on" came again and again.

....

watery soup didn't dampen my appetite soup that was mostly made of water did not make me less hungry

ease my weariness make me feel better

uneventful quiet, calm

Finally it ended. We were allowed to go to our barrack, where the food distribution line awaited us. I was at the point of fainting from hunger and fatigue. Fella was still in good spirits.

"It's beet jam again," she explained. **"Specialty of the house."**

It was food; that's all I cared about. If only there were a little more of it. The small portion hardly satisfied my hunger.

Fella went to see Regina, the *Blockälteste,* for permission to let me share the top bunk with her. "Quick," she told me afterward, "let's get your things before she changes her mind."

"A top bunk is safer," she said. "Well, we do get wet when it rains, but an angry night patrol has a harder time reaching up here."

I would have followed Fella anywhere, so happy was I to have found a friend. Holding my muddy shoes in one hand and my tin cup in the other, I climbed to the top bunk. Now I was finally able to do something about my sore hands. Ripping a strip of cloth off the hem of my dress, I **fashioned a bandage of sorts**.

The second day started out the same as the first. But then, at midmorning, Commandant Feix arrived at the workplace. He beat the guard with his riding whip, accusing him of being too **lenient** with the prisoners. According to Feix, we didn't work fast enough.

Life in this camp was strange. The torment of hard work, constant hunger, and **limited sanitary** conditions did nothing

....

"Specialty of the house." "The best food at camp."
fashioned a bandage of sorts wrapped my blisters
lenient kind, gentle
limited sanitary dirty, unclean

to **deter entrepreneurs**. Prisoners who still had contact with people on the outside were able to trade valuables for food or to **bribe** guards to let them have easier work.

Most of the trading was done in the main lane that went from one end of the camp to the other. It even had a name: Lagerstrasse.

Fella took me along one evening to show me how it was done. She knew lots of people and stopped many of them to find out where goods could be had. From others she inquired how the war was going, always clinging to the hope that it would soon be over.

Soon I, too, made it a practice to walk up and down Lagerstrasse each night, no matter how weary I was. I had no valuables to trade, but the walk was not intended for that. I was looking for Mama and Selly. I had already looked in all the women's barracks, and there was little chance I would find Mama. But I was hopeful about finding Selly. Then too the image of the man in the Polish army uniform, the one I had seen that first day, stayed with me. I thought about him often, hoping to see him again. Maybe he'd be walking along Lagerstrasse.

Fella and I became quite close. We told each other everything. I trusted her enough to cry in her arms over what had been done to me by that swine Schlesinger. We worried about each other. Seeing what a hard time I had walking in the wooden shoes given me, Fella led me to one of the

....

deter entrepreneurs stop the prisoners from starting trading businesses
bribe give things to the

99

women's barracks.

"I need a pair of shoes for my friend here," she said to a woman named Bronca.

Bronca looked at my feet to approximate their size and assured Fella **it was as good as done**. "Come back in a few days," she said. "It will cost you **a week's portion of bread**."

I looked on in amazement. "Where will we get the bread?" I asked.

"**Leave everything to me**," Fella said.

Our overseer, a Ukrainian *Kapo,* selected forty workers for what he called a "special project." Fella and I were among the forty. He led us into the forest, and the deeper we went the more fearful I became. It was no secret that Feix, our commandant, routinely shot people in the forest.

Alarmed at what was **in store for** us, Fella had the courage to ask the *Kapo,* "Sir, what kind of job are you taking us to? Why are we going so deep into the forest?"

He roared with laughter. "Don't worry, Feix isn't going to shoot you yet. He'll expect more work out of you first."

When we arrived at the thickest part of the forest, we stopped. The Ukrainian turned us over to another *Kapo* and left. Men and women worked side by side here. Men shoveled earth into ditches, while women used rakes to smooth the surface.

The new *Kapo* was not Ukrainian and he was friendly. "We know what happened here," he said in a hushed voice. "It's

....

it was as good as done she would get the shoes
a week's portion of bread all your bread this week
Leave everything to me I will take care of it
in store for going to happen to

unbearable to have to do this, yet we have no choice but to do as we are told. I'll try to be as understanding as I can be. Rest when you're tired, but don't get me into trouble. One of you has to **be on the lookout** at all times, making sure Feix is not nearby. Is that understood?"

Physically, the work was easy, but the thought of filling in a **mass grave**—and the smell, the unbearable smell of human decay—was too much to bear. Unspeakable thoughts occurred to me: What if Selly was in this mass grave? When the soup arrived, I was unable to eat even though I was terribly hungry.

"You *must* eat," Fella pleaded. But I would not **hear of it**.

"Eat in a *graveyard?*" With a wave of a hand I dismissed the subject of eating.

I failed to hear the approaching footsteps, but somehow I was compelled to look up. To my astonishment it was the man in the Polish army uniform.

He smiled at me. "I have been looking for you. You are the girl who came alone, without a transport."

My face reddened. If only he knew how often I had dreamt of seeing him. Now that he stood before me, I **was at a loss for words**.

"Don't you remember me?" he teased. "I was sure you would."

I could feel my cheeks burning. "It's . . . this place. It has me so upset. I am not myself right now," I said. "Ever since I arrived in Budzyn, I've been looking for my mother and my brother.

....

be on the lookout watch carefully
mass grave large hole with many dead bodies in it
hear of it listen to her
was at a loss for words did not know what to say

I was so sure I would find them in Budzyn, and now the most awful thought has occurred to me."

"Ah, little one, don't **jump to conclusions**. Just because you haven't seen them doesn't mean anything. Budzyn is a big camp."

I looked up into those beautiful eyes. What if he was right?

"Where are you from?" he wanted to know.

I told him about Aurich, how near it was to the North Sea and how far away it was from this place.

Then it was time for him to go back to work. A different guard had taken over, and we no longer had the same freedom. All afternoon I thought of the Polish soldier, and toward evening I saw him again.

"There is a small shed, right behind the kitchen," he whispered. "Will you meet me there tonight? Don't worry, it's safe."

My emotions **seesawed from** worry over Mama's and Selly's fate to the excitement of having met the Polish soldier again and how he had looked at me with those enchanting eyes. I remembered every word he said and could hardly wait to see him.

The door of the shed creaked. Cautiously, I went inside. It was dark, but I saw the **silhouette** of a man holding a mug in his hand.

"You came." He was obviously pleased. "Here!" He handed

....

jump to conclusions make judgements so quickly
seesawed from went back and forth between
silhouette shape, outline

me the mug. "Coffee. It's for you."

"Sweetened coffee!" I exclaimed after taking the first sip. "How did you manage that?"

"Eat and drink," he commanded, handing me a thick slice of bread.

I wanted to know where and how he had gotten these treasures, but he just laughed, ignoring my questions. He had questions of his own.

"Ever since that first night when I saw you, I've wondered why they **took the trouble** to bring in one person. I would have expected them to shoot you instead. Tell me what happened."

I hesitated.

"Come on, you can trust me."

In tears I blurted out the events that had taken place at Krašnik. I **held nothing back**. Finishing the story I said, "I'd wanted to believe him and convinced myself he was trying to help me. I made the mistake of ignoring **the danger signs**."

"Stop blaming yourself for trusting the Nazi. Anyone would have done the same," he said reassuringly. "You could not have guessed the outcome."

We parted with plans to meet again the next evening. I hurried back to the barrack.

"Fella, wait till you hear what happened to me!" I exclaimed to my friend.

"So, tell me already."

....

took the trouble worked so hard

held nothing back told him everything

the danger signs things he did or said that should have made me not trust him

"I think I am in love."

"The Polish soldier?"

"I met him tonight, in the shed behind the kitchen. He brought me bread and coffee. I don't mean the bitter stuff they give us; this was sweet and tasty. For once I am not hungry."

"How can you talk of love in a place like this?" Fella snapped. "One doesn't fall in love in a place like Budzyn."

"It's too late, darling Fella. Love is not something you plan, it just happens."

A bare lightbulb hanging from the ceiling cast shadows. The barrack was uncommonly quiet, but I was too excited to sleep. The young man had looked so handsome in his uniform, and up close his eyes were even more **magnetic**. Never before had I seen eyes like his. Somehow they reminded me of a **doe** I'd once surprised in the woods. Her dark, fluid eyes had looked at me for a **split second** before she fled into the underbrush. His eyes were like that.

This night the rough straw covering the bunk didn't irritate my skin as much, and there were no hunger pangs. The chunk of bread he had brought was almost as much as a week's portion, and I had eaten all of it.

The anticipation of seeing the Polish prisoner of war at work the next day made getting up at dawn not nearly as bad. However, nothing had changed in the forest. The **stench** of human decay remained, and the knowledge of being at a mass grave, having to disguise it, was no less horrible. But the

....

magnetic wonderful to look at
doe deer, animal
split second very short time
stench terrible smell

thought of seeing *him* made it bearable. Every now and then I caught him looking my way. At noon, when the soup was brought and we had time to rest for a short while, he walked over to where I sat and reminded me to come this evening to our meeting place.

When we went back to work, a woman who had been **toiling alongside** me suddenly moaned and grabbed the sleeve of my dress before collapsing to the ground. In the process she dragged me along.

Nothing escaped the guard. "Get up, you lazy swine," he growled.

I complied quickly, trying to lift the woman to her feet as well, but the guard put his rifle to my chest. "She'll get up by herself."

The woman was unable to move. The guard screamed more obscenities at the poor woman before **emptying his gun into** her.

In the evening I met him at the shed. Like the night before, he brought coffee and bread with margarine.

"I don't even know your name," I said, accepting the gifts.

"Call me Hillman, everyone else does," he replied jovially.

Still **traumatized** from what had happened in the forest, I told him how I detested having to stand by without being able to help the poor woman.

"I saw it," he said. "I know how you feel. Every time I am

....

toiling alongside working very hard next to
Nothing escaped the guard. The guard saw us.
emptying his gun into shooting and killing
traumatized feeling upset; shocked

in a situation like that, I hate myself for not helping, knowing full well that there is nothing I can do. It's not that we don't want to help, but we are helpless ourselves, imagine what the guard would have done to you had you **defied** his orders."

When it came time to part, he pulled a pair of socks and underwear from his pocket. I blushed at the sight of the intimate garments, but already I could feel their warmth against my cold body.

In spite of the danger of being discovered I met Hillman almost nightly at the shed behind the kitchen.

"It's your turn to tell me about your life," I urged him one evening.

I learned that he had been **conscripted into** the Polish armed forces in 1939 and shortly afterward was captured and sent to a German prisoner of war camp.

"I was in that **POW** camp nearly three years," he said. "I had typhoid fever and almost didn't make it. Only once did I try to escape, but the Germans caught me. They beat me so bad, I was unable to sit for many weeks.

His eyes had a far-off, dreamy look. Talking about that time seemed to take him back there. I knew it was painful for him to remember.

"You may as well tell me the rest," I said after a long silence. "How did you get to Budzyn?"

"No one at the POW camp knew I was a Jew. It wasn't as if

....

defied not listened to
conscripted into called by the government to join
POW Prisoner of War

I hid it deliberately, but Jewish prisoners **were singled out for** extra punishment, and the Poles . . . they were eager to do their part against us, too. They stole boots from Jews, making them walk barefoot in the cold of winter. So you can see why I didn't **own up to** who I was.

"One day the Germans made us an offer, announcing that all Jewish prisoners would be free to go home. I was eager to get back to my mother and sisters, knowing they could use my help, so I stepped forward."

"Had you heard from your family during those years?"

"Now and then a postcard came **via the Red Cross**. Mother wrote that my brother, Isio, was no longer at home. All the more reason for me to be with her. I should have known better than to believe the Germans. As soon as we stepped forward, they herded us onto trains, where SS men awaited us. We knew then that it had been a trick. I ended up here."

It was at that moment that I realized how deeply I had fallen in love with him.

"I have good news," he said, interrupting my thoughts. "Starting tomorrow I'll be working in the camp kitchen. My friend Medjuck arranged it. He's the cook."

....

were singled out for received
own up to tell anyone
via the Red Cross through a group who helped us

> **BEFORE YOU MOVE ON...**
>
> 1. **Evidence and Conclusions** Give examples from pages 100–105 that show the degradation Jewish people experienced.
>
> 2. **Tone** Reread pages 103–106. How did the tone change once Hannelore and the Polish soldier met?
>
> **LOOK AHEAD** Read pages 108–118 to learn why camp life was dangerously unpredictable.

chapter twelve

More good news: I learned that Dr. Mosbach and his family were here in Budzyn. I immediately **got my hopes up** and rushed to the infirmary to talk to him about the evacuation from Belzyce. Had he seen my family?

The doctor shook his head sadly. "There was a lot of confusion, and I was concerned about keeping my family together. I paid little attention to anything else."

My hopes shattered, I turned to walk away.

"Look here, Hannelore," he said, "I can well understand why you are sad. I wish I had more to tell you. But just because I didn't see your family doesn't mean anything. They may be working in another one of the labor camps."

Commandant Feix, the madman, was always **on the rampage, seizing every opportunity to torment us**. The danger

....

got my hopes up got excited and started to think that I might find my family

on the rampage, seizing every opportunity to torment us very angry and never missed a chance to hurt us

of encountering him during the day was constant, and an encounter with Feix was something every prisoner wanted to avoid. But we could not avoid him at night. He was there, every evening, at the place of assembly. One time the counting of prisoners took **exceptionally long**. Something was very wrong. *Kapos* ran back and forth, counting again and again.

Fella, her voice as low as she could make it, said, "I think someone escaped. That's why they are keeping us."

Feix started to scream. "Swine! Children of whores! Dirty Jews! I will keep you here until I know what happened. One of you has the answer. Come forward or all of you will suffer!"

It was so quiet, people forgot to breathe. Feix strutted among us women, **letting his riding whip dance freely over** our heads and other parts of our bodies. There was no mention of our evening ration or of going to the barracks to sleep for the few hours that remained before the morning whistle called us back for another count.

Drunk with rage, Feix kept us standing there. A full moon looked on, a witness to our misery. Then the madman rushed over to the men's side, pulling every tenth prisoner forward until he counted ten men.

"Let this be a lesson," his voice thundered. "For every one who tries to escape ten of you will die!"

Pulling out his revolver, he shot each of the men. Soon a pile of twitching bodies lay before us.

At last we were allowed into the barracks. Our evening

....

exceptionally long a very long time

letting his riding whip dance freely over hitting us with his riding whip on

Drunk with rage Because he was very angry

ration had been **forfeited** as punishment.

"Now you know why life in Budzyn is **like a game of roulette**," Fella said sourly.

Sickened by what I had just witnessed, I could not reply.

I didn't see Hillman the next evening or the one after. I had caught a cold and was barely able to make it through the day. I even had to give up my walk along Lagerstrasse to look for Mama and Selly.

When the cauldron of soup arrived the next day, Hillman carried it.

"Where have you been?" he asked. But **one look at me convinced him** I was ill. "You must come tonight to the shed. What you need is food and some warm clothing."

When evening came, I dragged myself to the shed. He was already there, waiting with a bowl of hot soup filled with vegetables.

"Eat while it's hot," he ordered. "We'll talk after."

It tasted like real soup, not the watery brew we were served. I felt better instantly. Then came the next surprise. He pulled a pair of boots and a sweater from under his jacket and held them out to me.

Suddenly everything seemed better. No longer so hungry and already feeling the warmth of the boots and sweater, I exclaimed. "To think, only a short time ago we were total

....

forfeited taken away from us
like a game of roulette never safe; uncertain
one look at me convinced him after he looked at me he knew that

strangers, and here you are now, risking being punished for bringing me these things. How can I ever thank you?"

"You should know by now why I am doing this," he said. Then he reminded me it was time to go back.

chapter thirteen

It was Sunday, the one day I didn't have to go to work. I got up early anyway to be one of the first people in the washroom. To be able to stand near the basin and have plenty of water before the supply was shut off was a luxury I did not want to miss.

At midmorning I took a walk along Lagerstrasse. Here and there I stopped to talk to people I had gotten to know. Quite unexpectedly, someone tapped me on the shoulder. Big brown eyes set in **hollow sockets** looked straight at me. The man was terribly thin . . . or perhaps it was a boy; it was hard to tell.

"Hannelore" was all he said.

How did he know my name? I didn't think I had ever met him before.

Again he said, "Hannelore."

The way he pronounced my name . . . *Selly?* No, it couldn't be my brother. Selly was young and handsome.

....

hollow sockets a very skinny face

"Don't you recognize me? Have I changed that much?"

"Dear God," I cried out. "It *is* you, Selly! You can't know how I have searched for you!"

I wanted to hug him, to hold him, but **held back, lest we** be noticed. To hide my shock at seeing him like this—emaciated, his clothes in tatters—I **prattled on**. "It's just that . . . you have grown so much. You're tall, like Papa."

But it wasn't only the way Selly looked that frightened me. He had a hard time breathing, and I could hear a rattling noise coming from his chest every time he coughed.

"Something to eat." He grabbed at my sleeve. "I need something, anything. You don't know how hungry I am!"

Fortunately, I had the extra bread Hillman had given me the night before in my pocket. When Selly was done eating, I tried taking his hands in mine. He pulled them back. His hands were full of open sores. I could only imagine how painful they must be.

I took him to the infirmary. Dr. Mosbach was as surprised as I to learn that Selly had been in Budzyn the entire time. He confirmed what I already knew.

"Your brother is **undernourished** and growing too fast. Add to that the collapsed lung he received from the beating in Belzyce. **Not a good picture.** How old is he, Hannelore?"

"F-Fifteen," I stammered.

Selly was admitted to the infirmary. Dr. Mosbach promised to keep him there as long as he possibly could.

....

held back, lest we did not so that we would not
prattled on talked about nothing important
undernourished not getting enough food
Not a good picture. He is very sick.

I went to see him each evening. From the infirmary I rushed to the shed to meet Hillman. By now I called him Dick, the name his comrades had **bestowed on** him. We had even kissed in the dark shed.

In spite of my feelings for Dick I was too troubled by my brother's condition to feel real happiness. Dick tried helping me as best he could. To **lighten my mood, he hummed arias** from operas. Most of the time I recognized the tunes, explaining that Papa, too, had liked opera and that oftentimes he would transpose the tunes into songs we sang on Friday nights to **usher in the Sabbath**.

"Tell me what you remember most about home," Dick asked me one evening.

"A lilac tree," I said. "It bloomed every May around the time of Mama's birthday. Papa was a romantic; he would stand under the tree and sing songs of lilacs and love to her. The memory is so vivid in my mind, I can almost smell the lilacs now."

"One day, when this is over, I'll plant you a lilac bush. Perhaps it will grow old and become a tree, like the one you remember."

"And we will run barefoot through the meadows," I added. "Just think of all the buttercups and other wildflowers we can gather along the way."

For that brief moment I allowed my heart to swell with joy.

....

bestowed on given to

lighten my mood, he hummed arias make me feel better, he sang songs

usher in the Sabbath begin our celebration of our holy day

chapter fourteen

Selly was released from the infirmary after one week. As much as Dr. Mosbach wanted to keep him, he simply couldn't.

"**Long-term illness** is not tolerated here," he said. "Twice they asked about him. He must leave immediately."

Selly had to go back to work the next day. I looked for him every evening and shared my food with him whenever I could, but he was too ill. Food alone could not save him. I didn't know **where to turn** or what to do. Day after day I feared for his safety, for it was well known that Feix **didn't spare anyone** who was not **robust** enough to work. Prisoners who failed to meet his standards were led into the forest, never to be seen again.

A coworker told me one morning that she had just seen another group of prisoners being led into the forest. A group of *Musselmen*, she called them—emaciated prisoners who could no longer work. I was scared that Selly might be among them.

....

Long-term illness Being sick for a long time
where to turn where to get help
didn't spare anyone did not keep anyone alive
robust strong, healthy

Leaving my work site at the great risk of being punished, I ran into the square, where Feix was **holding court**. Never before had I **possessed the courage** to go near him. Trying to make my voice as steady as I possibly could, I addressed him.

"Herr Untersturmführer, allow me to talk to you. My brother has mistakenly been taken away. He is a young boy; he can work."

"And who are you?" he asked.

"My name is Hannelore Wolff."

"You speak proper German. Where are you from?"

"Ostfriesland, Herr Untersturmführer."

"And your brother's name?"

"Selly Wolff."

Turning to one of his aides, Feix shouted, "Find Selly Wolff. Bring him here."

I stood waiting, hoping Feix would not notice how frightened I was, how much my body shook with fear.

The aide appeared a short time later with Selly **in tow**. His eyes bulging with fright, dressed in tattered clothes, and pitifully thin, he looked indeed like a *Musselman*.

Now Feix would see I had lied to him. There was no **telling** what he would do. Perhaps he would kill us both, make an example of us by hanging us.

Then an amazing thing happened. Feix ordered his aide to take Selly to the infirmary with instructions that he be given double rations. For the first time in a long while I believed that

....

holding court talking to some of the prisoners
possessed the courage been brave enough
in tow walking behind him
telling way to know

God might still be watching over us.

Later that day, after work, I went to see Selly in the infirmary. "What did you say to Feix?" he asked. "Many people had already been shot. Had the aide come a few minutes later, I would have **faced the same fate**."

"I told him you were young and could work. I think he was surprised to hear me speak German. I don't know why he did it. We both know he is a madman. Why does he do these terrible things to human beings day after day?"

Selly had nothing to fear from the daily inspections of SS men. They didn't even bother to look at him, and there was no talk of releasing him from the infirmary. But the truth was that Selly was extremely ill. I continued to visit him every evening. And every evening I noticed **rapid** changes—the **rattling breath**, the pleading for water. I understood the seriousness of the situation and begged one of the hospital workers to let me stay on a night that Selly was especially bad and kept calling for me to please give him more water.

"Why would I risk my job when anyone can see he is **not going to make it**?" the aide asked.

"That's why I am pleading with you. Let him have the comfort of having me here. I will give you my bread portion for a week. Please, let me stay, just this once!"

"Who needs your bread?" he shouted angrily. "Get away from here before you get me into trouble."

Walking away, I could still hear Selly's cries for water.

....

faced the same fate also been shot
rapid quick
rattling breath hard time he had breathing
not going to make it going to die

The next morning my dear brother was dead.

Life in Budzyn got even tougher. There was a shortage of food and our rations were cut further. The already watery soup had fewer turnips and beets in it. The guards turned more sullen and were less forgiving of minor offenses. Even the weather turned against us: It was bitter cold.

I noticed a change in Dick Hillman as well. He seemed preoccupied, withdrawn.

"You are absent even when you're with me," I said.

He did not deny it. After a brief silence he told me that Jews all over Europe were being **rounded up**, and that was of great concern.

"So many people arrive here every day," he added. "Soon Budzyn will not hold all of us."

He is preparing me for what is to come, I thought with alarm. *What if we are sent to different camps? What if I never see him again?*

"If it is any consolation," he continued, trying to make me feel better, "the war is not going well for the Germans. But it's not over yet. Have you noticed that the younger guards here have been replaced with older ones? All the young soldiers are being sent to the Russian front."

"How do you know all this?" I asked.

"It's . . . it's something I can't share with you. Hannelore, please don't ask again."

....

rounded up taken to camps

BEFORE YOU MOVE ON...

1. **Simile** Reread page 110. Why did Fella compare life in Budzyn to "a game of roulette"?

2. **Conclusions** Reread page 114. Why was the lilac tree important to Hannelore?

LOOK AHEAD Read pages 119–129 to see how the war affected religious beliefs.

chapter fifteen

By the time news of the heavy fighting between Germany and Russia reached us, Feix had already left. We presumed he had been shipped to the Russian front. We soon had a new commandant. His name was Joseph Liebholt. He was tough but not as crazy and irrational as Feix had been. The speech he delivered on his first day let us know what to expect.

"Only working people are entitled to food. **Freeloaders** are not tolerated. **Saboteurs will be shot on the spot.** Should you at any time entertain the idea of escape, you will regret it. Your fellow inmates will pay with *their* lives for it."

But from the first Liebholt **gave preferential treatment** to the Polish prisoners of war, installing them in better positions. While Dick remained in the kitchen, others were installed as *Blockältestes*—or overseers. As far as I knew, all the prisoners of war at Budzyn were Jewish.

Freeloaders People who do not work

Saboteurs will be shot on the spot. People who cause trouble will be killed immediately.

gave preferential treatment was nicer

The harsh winter of 1943 came to an end, and it was spring again. Fella worked at a construction site where members of the German Wehrmacht—ordinary soldiers—guarded the inmates. These soldiers had been returned from the Russian front to trade places with young SS men who could fight with more **vigor**.

"You'll be surprised how much friendlier these people are," Fella told me one day. "I wish the Ukrainian *Kapos* would go away, though."

Then Fella produced a piece of chocolate a German soldier had given her. She had saved it for me.

"It tastes heavenly," I said after finishing it off quickly, "but promise not to bring chocolate into camp again. It's too dangerous. What if they'd **had one of the random searches** at the gate? How would you explain a piece of chocolate?"

"You worry too much, Hannelore. Why would they search me? I look harmless."

Then it occurred to me that Fella had not been entirely honest. Why would a German soldier give her chocolate?

"Are you flirting with these men?"

Fella laughed her deep, carefree laugh. "Hannelore, you know me better than anyone in this world. It's so much fun to flirt. It almost makes me feel like a normal person. These men **are starved for affection**. They have just come from the Russian front and haven't been around women for a long time. There is one soldier, the one who gave me the chocolate. I like

....

vigor energy, strength

had one of the random searches decided to look through your things

are starved for affection want women to pay attention to them

him best. He is handsome . . . blond hair, blue eyes. He is not afraid to talk to—"

"You are out of your mind talking to a German soldier!" I interrupted her heatedly. "No good can come of that."

"He told me how much it upsets him having to guard us. He wanted me to know how he **deplores** what's going on here."

"And that makes it all right for you to flirt with him? Wake up, Fella. Better yet, promise you will stop talking to him."

Aside from the usual hardships of not having enough to eat and standing for hours at the place of assembly before and after a long day's work, the camp remained as before. Yet there was **an underlying quiet, like one that often precedes a storm**. Dick seemed even more preoccupied than usual. He was always in a rush to get away. One evening I held him back.

"Please, tell me what's going on. I get the feeling you don't love me anymore."

"Of course I love you, Hannelore. My own feelings have nothing to do with this. But there are things I can't share with you right now. You'll have to accept that."

When he didn't come to our meeting place the next night. I was alarmed. I shuddered to think what would happen if he belonged to **an underground movement** and were found out. The commandant would have him hanged.

I remembered only too well the hangings of five young men who allegedly belonged to such a movement. It happened only

....

deplores hates

an underlying quiet, like one that often precedes a storm something wrong, and it seemed too quiet

an underground movement a secret group that opposed the Nazis

days after my arrival in Budzyn. These young men were hung upside down to prolong their agony. I tried to forget the scene, but it wasn't easy.

Night after night I waited for Dick. No one had seen him. I turned to Fella, who was well connected and found out things few people knew.

"You've got to help me!" I pleaded.

But in the ensuing days I had the feeling that Fella, too, was avoiding me.

"Tell me what you know," I said. "Don't you realize that not knowing is torture?"

"I warned you about falling in love. If you didn't love him so much, you wouldn't have to worry now."

"Worry about *what?*"

"He is being held for . . . questioning."

"What about? What did he do?"

"He has connections to the **partisans** on the outside. Someone found out and has been **blackmailing him for some time**. In the end the man **turned Dick in**. And since Untersturmführer Liebholt is in Berlin, there is nothing to be done. Liebholt will not allow anyone's interference in Budzyn matters. We'll have to wait and see."

"They'll beat him to death first!" I cried.

"He is a brave man, Hannelore. He was aware of the risk."

I began to pray, asking God to take care of not myself, but the man I loved so deeply. Dick himself was no longer a

....

partisans people who were against the Nazis

blackmailing him for some time forcing Dick to give him money not to tell the Nazis about Dick's connections

turned Dick in told the Nazis what Dick was doing

religious man. He told me that once he was a believer. He had been raised in an Orthodox house, had studied with a **rebbe** for many years. But that was then, he said. He found it meaningless now. He often wondered how much faith I had in God.

"I can't prove to you that there is a God, I just know," I had told him. "All this suffering has to have a reason."

Three days passed without any news about Dick. On the third evening I walked along Lagerstrasse hoping to hear something about **his whereabouts**. One of the prisoners who shared his barrack came up behind me and said, "Keep walking. Good news: Hillman is free. It happened a few hours ago, after Liebholt came back."

"Thank God he is alive!"

"They **roughed** him up. He is in bad shape, but we'll **get him back on his feet**."

....

rebbe Jewish teacher
his whereabouts where Dick was
roughed beat
get him back on his feet help him get better

chapter sixteen

"Look at you, **you're wasting away**," Fella told me one night. "Soon you'll be a *Musselman*. So Dick refuses to see you. He must have good reason."

"If only I knew why," I said.

"Can't you forget about him for one evening? I looked forward to sharing this good food, but with you acting so miserable, all the pleasure is gone. Just look at this: cheese, salami, and bread. Eat! You'll feel better."

I never missed my nightly walk along Lagerstrasse, no matter how tired and depressed I was. Finally I saw Dick. His head was bandaged, his eyes **bloodshot and swollen**.

"My God, what did they do to you?" I cried.

"Keep walking," he ordered. "Pretend you don't know who I am. We'll be leaving Budzyn soon. The camp is being

....

you're wasting away you look sick

bloodshot and swollen were red and larger than normal because he had been hit in the face

liquidated. I thought you should know." He sounded grim, **despondent**.

Before I had a chance to say anything else, he was gone.

Back in my barrack I discovered Fella had not returned yet. This was the third time this week that my **bunkmate** had stayed out after curfew. Much later, after everyone was asleep, she appeared.

"You're late again," I snapped, upset with my friend for taking unnecessary risks.

Fella was not her usual self. As soon as she reached the top bunk, she began to cry.

"I am in love with the German soldier, and he is in love with me," she told me. "What am I going to do?"

"You think you're in love because he gives you food and he treats you nice. But he is a *German*! Don't you see how **impossible the situation is**? Fella, please think about the danger you're putting yourself in!"

Ever since Dick had told me that we would leave Budzyn soon, I carried all I owned with me. The tin cup, a comb, and, of course, my most precious possession: the few pictures from home. What I worried about was not knowing whether I would ever see Dick again.

Then, one afternoon, we were told to line up at the place of assembly. That meant only one thing to me: The time had come—we were leaving Budzyn, just as Dick had predicted.

....

despondent very unhappy; hopeless
bunkmate friend
impossible the situation is you two could never be together

As usual, we stood in lines of five waiting to be counted. The *Blockälteste* walked up and down, counting and recounting. Something wasn't right. Suddenly I knew what it was. Fella was not here! Fella had always stayed close by me at the place of assembly. Where could she be? This was too important an order to ignore.

Afternoon turned to evening, and still we waited. Searchlights circled overhead and SS men guided sniffing dogs around on leashes. Then Liebholt appeared, **unkempt and unshaven**, his eyes flashing with anger. The drama of the evening was heightened by his shrill voice.

"Damn you, Jew pigs! What made you think you could **corrupt a German soldier** and get away with it?"

The moment he said that, I knew what this was all about. His voice rose to a new pitch: "Barrack six, on your knees. Put your heads down."

The ground was soft from recent rain. My knees sank deeper and deeper into the mud; the blood drained to my head. Yet I dared not look up for fear of being punished by the guards.

Our release came many hours later, in the morning, when the whistle **for roll call** sounded. There was still no sign of Fella.

....

unkempt and unshaven he looked dirty and had not shaved

corrupt a German soldier get a German soldier to fall in love with you

for roll call calling us to be counted

chapter seventeen

Weeks passed, and still we remained in Budzyn. No one knew for sure what had happened to Fella. But by putting the rumors together, **a picture emerged**. Evidently, her friendship with the German soldier had been discovered, and the two had been punished for it. The soldier had been sent back to the Russian front; Fella had been beaten to death. The thought of my friend's horrible end was heartbreaking for me. I missed her so much. Day after day I cried for her.

I saw Dick only occasionally. He still had not recovered from the beating, but the bruises on his face looked less fierce now.

One evening he arrived at our meeting place carrying something **bulky** under his coat. "A present for you," he said. When he pulled out a pair of black boots and told me to put them on, I cried with joy at the prospect of having warm feet.

....

a picture emerged we were able to guess what happened
bulky big

The look on his face soon dampened my spirits.

"This might be the last thing I can do for you, little one," he said. "I wish it didn't have to be. I have never met anyone like you. The little village we lived in didn't have very many girls but sometimes my older brother, Isio, took me along on his dates after we left the village to live in a big city. His friends were **idealists**, full of hope for a better tomorrow. Long after I was inducted into the army, they still sang their songs about freedom."

I had not seen or heard him like this before, so sorrowful, so **melancholic**.

"I often think about Isio and his friends and wonder where they are," he continued. "My mother, my sisters, God only knows what happened to them!"

"Is this . . . farewell?" I asked, fearful of his answer.

"For now it is. But I promise I will find you, wherever you are."

When SS units surrounded the camp to seal it and we were ordered to the place of assembly, I knew we were leaving. My back stiffened and my legs cramped up. I wanted to remember where this terrible place was so I could come back one day to visit Selly's grave. The thought of my young brother in a mass grave **started me sobbing**. I struggled to control myself.

The loudspeaker blared out orders as the first column of prisoners marched out of the gate. I turned one more time to

....

idealists people who believed they could make the world a better place

melancholic full of sadness

started me sobbing made me cry

look for Dick, but **he was nowhere in sight**. Guards hurried me toward the station and the waiting **cattle cars**, a painful reminder of my trip from Weimar with Mama and my brothers.

The train moved through the night, its wheels clanking monotonously on the rails. The crammed car offered no comforts. When morning came and the first rays of light entered through the cracks, the train stopped.

We had reached the next station along our journey through hell.

....

he was nowhere in sight I could not see him

cattle cars trains that usually carried cows

We had reached the next station along our journey through hell. We reached the next camp where we knew we would continue to suffer and die.

BEFORE YOU MOVE ON...

1. **Conclusions** Reread pages 122–123. Why did Dick lose his religious faith while Hannelore continued to rely on hers?

2. **Inference** Why did Fella continue to meet with the German soldier even though it was dangerous?

LOOK AHEAD Read pages 130–144 to find out how Dick disappointed Hannelore.

chapter eighteen

SS men unbolted the cattle cars, ordering us to jump out. One of them, a burly man, was about to strike me on the head for not obeying fast enough. I put my hands up to protect myself.

"Get your hands down, you pig!" he yelled, hitting me hard.

I held back the tears **welling up**. The pain was intense and so was the nagging hunger. There had been no food or water on the train. If Fella were here, she would have uttered a **wisecrack** to make light of this situation. How I missed her.

A sign at the station announced that this was Wieliczka, home of the Polish **salt mines**. Terrified of what was in store for us next, I spotted Untersturmführer Liebholt. Arrogant as ever, he stood before us, legs spread apart.

"The easy days of Budzyn are over for you. Here you'll learn what the word *work* means. I will keep you working in the mines until you beg to come out. The sight of you offends me.

....

welling up that formed in my eyes
wisecrack joke
salt mines pits under the ground filled with salt

You smell like swine!"

He went on with his ravings, but I stopped listening to him. He was trying to **break our morale—or what was left of it**.

I noticed that only five of the cars had been **uncoupled**. The rest of the train had not been touched. It soon left the station. And so it was that only a few hundred of us were marched up the mountains, where wildflowers bloomed. It was a pretty sight, especially after the drab Budzyn camp, and it felt good to breathe fresh air.

This camp was different. The absence of barbed-wire fences and watchtowers was a welcome change. The men's and women's barracks were adjacent to each other and allowed for conversation and some kind of friendship, and there was more room on the bunks. I headed for the washroom and discovered there was water, plenty of it. I drank **to my heart's content**.

I walked around the camp looking for Dick. Before long I encountered one of the Polish prisoners of war. My hopes soared. If this man was here, so too might be all the rest of the POWs.

"Where can I find Hillman?" I asked him.

"I don't know," he answered. "Only four hundred of us are needed here, and only for a few months. We will be replaced by Polish laborers when they return from working in Germany."

"Surely Hillman is here. Are you trying to tease me?"

"Don't be absurd. Why would I tease you?"

The man proceeded to tell me that the rest of our transport had gone on to a camp called Plaszow. We would be going

....

break our morale—or what was left of it make us feel worse than we already did

uncoupled separated and unloaded

to my heart's content as much water as I wanted

there too as soon as our work here was finished. In the meantime I should be glad to be here. As bad as Liebholt was, the commandant in Plaszow was much worse, the soldier said. He went on to warn me to be careful when I went down in the mines. It was dark and easy to get lost there.

"Once, when I was a young boy, my father brought me here. He did business in this area. I was taken down into a mine. At the time it was an adventure. Now . . ."

Slowly, I walked back to the women's barrack. I felt alone and unprotected without Dick. An angry *Blockälteste* greeted me. "Where have you been?" she snapped.

"I was searching for a friend," I answered.

"Liebholt was looking for you. He got mad at me when I couldn't find you."

I felt the blood draining from my face. "Liebholt? Why was he looking for me?"

"You'll be working for him. His mistress wants a German-speaking maid. Report to his residence tomorrow morning."

Having to **come face-to-face with** this evil man nearly made me **reel**. I begged the *Blockälteste* to pick someone else.

"Are you crazy? Going against Liebholt's orders is like **signing your own death warrant**."

All night long the vision of Liebholt dogged me. Unable to sleep, I pretended that I was still home with Mama and Papa and that it was the month of May. The lilac tree in our yard was in

....

come face-to-face with stand in front of; meet

reel fall over

signing your own death warrant asking somebody to kill you

bloom, its branches so full that they curved downward under their heavy burden. Mama had **pruning shears** in her hand, while I held a crystal vase to be filled with the heavily scented lilacs. Papa, Wolfgang, and Selly sat on a bench nearby, planning Mama's birthday party. I knew it was all a fantasy, but it helped me cope with my anxiety.

Early the next morning I went to the washroom. No one was there. It was such a relief to not have to push myself through hundreds of women to get near the basin before the water stopped coming. I washed myself **at leisure** and felt cleaner than I had in a long time.

As I walked across the lawn to my new job I nervously adjusted and readjusted the faded print dress I had been given to wear.

Liebholt and his mistress lived in one of the villas across from the camp. I found it right away: JOSEPH LIEBHOLT, THIRD FLOOR. Upon entering the house, I noticed a faded mark on the **doorpost**. I knew what it meant. The mark showed the place where a mezuzah had once hung—a small box that contains **scrolled verses** from the Bible. Jews all over the world placed a mezuzah at the entrance to their houses. A shiver went through my body as I realized I was entering a Jewish house, now occupied by a Nazi.

How well I remembered the mezuzah that had hung on our doorpost. Before leaving Weimar, Mama had insisted we remove the box. "The Nazis will **desecrate** it," she had said.

....

pruning shears scissors to cut the branches
at leisure slowly
doorpost side of the frame around the door
scrolled verses written sayings
desecrate damage, destroy

I had dug a hole in the ground, wrapped the mezuzah in one of Papa's linen handkerchiefs, and buried it. I wondered if the people who had lived here had done the same.

The house was well cared for except for a wall in the stairwell where the wallpaper had been ripped off and empty bottles were **embedded in hollowed-out** holes in the wall. The former residents must have tried to hide their valuables in those bottles. However well hidden, the Nazis had obviously discovered them.

My hand was barely off the buzzer to the third floor residence when Liebholt, dressed in a maroon gown, opened the door. Without his uniform he looked different but no less **formidable**.

"I am Hannelore Wolff," I said, making my voice sound strong. "The *Blockälteste* sent me."

Liebholt motioned me inside, where I was left standing for some time. Laughter came through the door, and I was sure it was about me. Liebholt reappeared in a few minutes in his Nazi uniform. "Your mistress is waiting for you," he said.

Fräulein Liselotte did not **bid me hello**. Her first words were "There is no hot water on the third floor, so you'll have to fetch it from the cellar. You'll find two pails in the kitchen. And hurry I'm late for the club."

Pails in hand, I went down the three flights of stairs to the boiler room. I made many trips up and down until the tub was filled.

"Hold the towel for me," my mistress ordered.

....

embedded in hollowed-out pushed into
formidable scary, frightening
bid me hello say hello to me

After bathing and perfuming herself, the fräulein demanded her breakfast. I had never made coffee in my life and didn't know much about preparing bacon and eggs. I had never even seen bacon before. The fräulein scolded me a few times, asking why it took so long.

Finally my mistress **was off** to the club, leaving me with instructions about cleaning the apartment and getting dinner ready. I worked hard that day, yet she was not pleased. Upon her return she found fault with almost everything. After a few days of similar incidents she took her complaints to the *Untersturmführer.*

"The girl **is insolent**," I heard her say. "By the time she brings the last of the bathwater, my bath is already cold."

The next morning Liebholt ordered me to go down to the boiler room to bring the bathwater up. I walked as fast as I could with a pail in each hand. Up and down I went. On my third trip up he was waiting for me at the top of the stairs, placing himself in my way and deliberately tripping me. I stood in a puddle of water. My dress and shoes were soaked.

"You idiot. I told you to bring *hot* water. Look at you— you're not **scalded** as I expected you to be. You defied my orders."

I was **on the verge of crying** but managed to say, "I can explain, Herr Untersturmführer—"

"I didn't ask for explanations! All I want from you is to obey orders. Do your work or I will throw you out this window."

....

was off went
is insolent does not do what I tell her to do
scalded burned
on the verge of crying about to cry

I worked throughout the day, my wet clothes clinging to my body. I removed my shoes and walked in bare feet. When Fräulein Liselotte left for the club, I could have taken some of the leftover food to eat, but I was no longer hungry. At the end of the day I was dismissed.

The next day I started working in the mines. The crew I was assigned to went down the deep shaft in an elevator. **Save for** some flickering blue lights the mine was dark, and it took my eyes some time to get used to the darkness. I was cold and shivered in my thin dress.

I lingered behind the others, not knowing where to look first. The place was unreal. It was designed to look like an underground park, with lakes and walkways and carefully planted shrubbery. The huge walls—salt walls—looked as majestic as mountains. **I was totally absorbed in my observations** when I suddenly remembered what the Polish prisoner of war had told me: how easy it was to get lost in a mine. I hurried to join the rest of my group.

Just as I was about to pick up a shovel someone was handing me, I saw a **spine-chilling** creature dressed in black emerge from behind a trapdoor. My screams pierced the mine, echoing throughout. But I was the only one screaming; the others were used to the appearance of the foreman.

It was damp in the mine. Some of us worked, assembling parts for Germany's airplane industry. Others, like me, shoveled

....

Save for Other than
was totally absorbed in my observations had slowed down and was looking carefully at everything
spine-chilling scary, frightening

salt onto trucks. It **took its toll**. Adding to my fatigue was a constant pain under my rib cage. At first I attributed it to sore muscles, but when I was unable to eat, I knew it had to be something more serious.

One day the overseer saw me doubling over with pain. He wanted to know what was wrong. I hastened to say that it was nothing. But the truth was that the pain had been intensifying more and more each day. Afraid of going to the camp's infirmary, where I knew I wouldn't be safe, I decided to confide in a Jewish doctor who worked in the mine **giving first aid**.

Dr. Weiss was a kind man. He listened to my complaint, examined my eyes, and noted the color of my skin.

"What you describe sounds like a **gallbladder condition**," he said. "Under ordinary circumstances I would say you're too young for that, but living in camps as long as you have, anything is possible. A proper diet and not having to work underground in a salt mine would be my first recommendation. We both know that is not possible. Let me talk to the foreman. We understand each other. I'll ask him to let you work in the airplane factory down here. It will be easier than shoveling salt onto trucks."

The work in the factory part of the mine was indeed easier but still a struggle. It took as much **willpower as I could muster** to make it through each day.

Our provisions came from Plaszow since Wieliczka was a subcamp of Plaszow. Occasionally, letters were smuggled in

....

took its toll hurt my body
giving first aid helping people who were sick
gallbladder condition problem near your stomach
willpower as I could muster strength as I had

with the provisions. One day I received a note from Dick telling me how lucky I was to be in Wieliczka and instructing me not to volunteer to come to Plaszow just because he was there. *If you thought Feix was bad,* he wrote, *wait till you meet Amon Goeth. He is a **sadist of the worst kind**.*

I missed Dick terribly. Our meetings had been the one thing to look forward to each day. Without him I was often depressed. The pain in my back and abdomen had not gotten better, and I was afraid it would only be a matter of time before the foreman reported me for poor work performance. But he left me alone.

We had been in Wieliczka several months when **rumor had it** that Polish workers had arrived to replace us. Within a few days' time we were put on trucks to be transferred to the next camp, presumably Plaszow. As Dick had indicated in his note to me, this was not a good place to be. But I was not prepared for what awaited me. The place was huge. Wooden barracks extended for miles, and I could only guess how many prisoners it might take to fill them. Once inside, I saw **skeletons who resembled human beings** walking from one end of the barbed-wire complex to the other chanting, "Bread, a piece of bread. Have mercy on me!"

Other prisoners in striped uniforms took us into a barrack where I was told to kneel so they could cut off my hair. Swiftly, my shiny black hair fell to the floor. My hands went up, touching the uneven stubble. I kept thinking, *Mama and Papa would not be able to recognize me now,* forgetting again that Papa

....

sadist of the worst kind *very cruel person*
rumor had it the other prisoners started to say
skeletons who resembled human beings very skinny and sick looking people

was no longer alive and God only knew where Mama was.

We were herded into a large shower chamber next. All my belongings had to be left on a bench. *Not my pictures,* I vowed. *No, I will hold them in the palm of my hands.* I didn't believe they would give me my clothes back, especially the warm boots Dick had procured for me; but the pictures, the pictures had to stay with me always.

And so it was. When I emerged at the other end of the chamber, I was issued different clothes—a fancy evening dress and wooden shoes too big to walk in. The odd combination made me smile in spite of the horror of the situation. But my **initiation into** Plaszow was not complete yet. My forearm had to be tattooed. I quickly changed lines to be in Dr. Mosbach's. I was so happy to see him again.

"Suck this out as soon as I am finished," he whispered. "But first you must memorize the number. **Your name no longer matters**, it will be your number that will get you food and a bunk to sleep on."

I followed his advice and sucked on my forearm until there was no trace of the tattoo.

I joined other women wandering along the barbed-wire fence. Shouts of recognition **evoked** laughter from some and tears from others, but I could not find Dick among the men on the opposite side. The curfew whistle signaled that it was time to go to the barracks. I quickly found my way to my assigned bunk in one of the women's barracks and soon fell asleep.

....

initiation into arrival at; welcome to
Your name no longer matters No one will call you by your name here
evoked brought out

Another whistle awakened me. For a moment I didn't know where I was. In a fit of panic I ran to the entrance dressed in my evening gown and wooden shoes.

"Going to a **ball**?" the *Blockälteste* mocked. "Why didn't you have your hair styled more fashionably?"

"Oh dear God," I moaned, putting my hands on the uneven stubble that had once been a head of hair.

And that's how I went to work—dressed for a ball and accompanied by Ukrainian guards.

The work site smelled of burned flesh. Was this another mass grave, only much larger than the one in Budzyn?

"**Hard to take**, isn't it?" a girl standing next to me said in perfect German. "By the way, my name is Eva. What's yours?"

Eva was tall and slender and very attractive. She had an infectious laugh and the same charm Fella had had. I liked her immediately.

"Can you believe this?" I said. "I am dressed in a ball gown to **cover up evidence of mass murder**. Has the world gone mad?"

We had to stop talking. The Ukrainian guard came around handing out rakes. He was a mean-looking man.

"Anyone too lazy to work can tell me now. We'll take care of it right away. There is plenty of room left in those pits."

His instructions were to smooth out the earth, make it "nice-looking," he said. "Then no one will know the difference."

....

ball fancy party

Hard to take It is hard to be here and do this work

cover up evidence of mass murder hide the hundreds of dead people killed by Germans

I was so happy to have found Eva. She was a few years older than me. Originally from Stettin, she knew Dr. Mosbach and his family well. She even knew Eugen, the *Judenrat* policeman from Belzyce. They had been deported together. And it turned out that Eva, too, had worked for Untersturmführer Liebholt and his mistress. Fräulein Liselotte had had no complaints about Eva's work.

"I'm glad to have found someone who speaks German," she said. "Let's be friends." We shook hands and smiled.

The work was not too difficult, but the site and the smell of burned flesh were far worse than hard work. Both of us wondered how many pits there were to be found in the different camps and how human beings, prisoners like us, **came to end up this way**. Would it be our turn soon?

As the day **wore on** and the guard wandered away I had the courage to look over to where the men were working. I recognized some of the Budzyn men, and it gave me hope that Dick would be among them. When a few of the male prisoners crossed the women's path, I thought I heard a familiar voice.

"I . . . can't take it anymore." The voice was **barely audible**. "No lilac tree."

Before I could answer, Dick Hillman was gone.

From then on I saw him walking by every day. He worked the night shift, I the day shift. Sometimes our eyes met. He seemed infinitely sad, dejected, no longer the charismatic young man I had known. How I wished I could cheer him up.

....

came to end up this way had died this horrible death
wore on passed
barely audible hard to hear

He seemed to shrink from week to week. Every time the inspection whistle sounded, I was afraid he would be the one selected to die. The dreaded inspections took place often. Shrill whistles would **puncture our sleep, rousing us** at all hours of the night. Each time I made myself stand erect to give the appearance of being healthy. I even pinched my cheeks to make them look red before walking naked through the center of the barrack for inspection. Eva pricked her finger and would rub the blood into her cheeks. I lived in fear of these inspectors, knowing they could **condemn me at their whim**.

Dick had clearly lost his will to live. His eyes gave him away. And here I was, in constant pain and unable to digest the little food I was given, yet I was not ready to give up.

One of the male prisoners slipped me a note one morning, but it wasn't until nightfall that I was able to take it out of my wooden shoe and read it.

Little one, Our dream of being together one day is fading rapidly. I can't fight any longer. If only I could hold you in my arms once more.

I wept as I read Dick's note over and over, wondering what had **set off his deep** depression. He had risked his life so many times to help others. He was used to hunger and sickness. How could this have happened to him?

I walked over to Eva's bunk to share my sorrow with her.

....

puncture our sleep, rousing us wake us up

condemn me at their whim decide I should die whenever
they wanted to

set off his deep made him feel so much

She was good at consoling and counseling and **approved of my plan to hold Dick to** his promise.

And that's what I did. The following day I slipped a note to one of the Budzyn men, asking him to give the note to Dick.

What has come over you? You made me a promise. I am not releasing you from it. Come to the fence on Sunday.

When Sunday came, he was there. I saw tears in his eyes.

"I promised you to stay strong while we were apart," I said. "I expected the same from you. What happened?"

"I wish I could be like you now. At times I fear I have lost my mind." Even his voice was listless.

"It was you who warned me that things would get tougher."

"It's not the harsh conditions. My state of mind has to do with the work I do and losing so many of my comrades. We made it through five difficult years, and now . . . they are dead!"

I remained quiet so he could **get it all out**.

"Do you know what I do all night long? I violate the dead. I lift their **corpses** out of the pit, take gold teeth out of their mouths, then toss their bodies into the fire."

I could barely breathe. I was stunned.

"They give us double rations of bread for this work, but who can eat? What if some day I recognize one of the corpses? I don't know what I will do then!"

....

approved of my plan to hold Dick to thought it was a good idea to make Dick keep

get it all out say everything that he wanted to say

corpses dead bodies

I wanted to scream, *What kind of world is this?* Instead I told him, "You can't give up. I won't let you!"

I knew of the beatings and hangings that went on. I had seen them too often already. But I didn't know about mass graves **of these proportions** or of violating the dead by removing their gold teeth. . . . All I could think of was that the world had gone mad.

Dick was still standing near the fence. "There is a rumor going around," he said. "A man by the name of Oskar Schindler is taking eleven hundred Jews out of here. If only we could go with them."

I was about to ask him the details of this plan, but footsteps approached and a burly Ukrainian guard **loomed** nearby, ready to strike Dick with his **truncheon**. We both fled.

"Yids!" The Ukrainian laughed, chasing Dick until he disappeared in the crowd.

....

of these proportions that were this large
loomed appeared
truncheon stick, club

BEFORE YOU MOVE ON...

1. **Paraphrase** What did Dick mean when he said "No lilac tree"? What changed that made him feel this way?

2. **Irony** Reread page 137. What was ironic about Hannelore's comment about the infirmary being unsafe?

LOOK AHEAD Read pages 145–158 to find out what gave prisoners hope.

chapter nineteen

Searchlights revolved like spinning wheels, as if **setting the stage** for an evening of entertainment. But the situation was far from entertaining.

Loudspeakers blared orders for prisoners to undress. Another one of the feared inspections was taking place. My heart beat faster and faster. Would I pass this time? I joined the line of naked women being inspected by white-gloved SS officers.

"Move sideways . . . bend down . . . turn around," they shouted as they touched our naked bodies with their riding whips. One of them carried a **ledger** in which he wrote down numbers and names.

When it was my turn, nothing was written down. I had passed. For now I was safe. But too many numbers were recorded that night, and the atmosphere was **somber**. Thank God, Eva's number had not been written down.

....

setting the stage preparing; getting ready
ledger book
somber sad, serious

I worried about Dick and whether he had passed. The conversation we'd had at the fence came back to me. He talked about a man who was taking eleven hundred prisoners away from here. I had forgotten his name. If only we could go with those prisoners, away from this awful place. I fell asleep dreaming of leaving Plaszow.

Loud voices coming from a lower bunk awakened me.

"You stole my bread, you thief!"

"Listen to her," another responded. "She is going mad. She ate her bread, and now she is blaming me."

"Give me back what you stole," the girl called Riva said. She sounded like a wounded animal.

The curtain to the *Blockälteste*'s cubicle parted. Dressed in a flimsy nightgown, the *Blockälteste* rushed forward, followed by a man.

"Who is responsible for this?" The woman's thundering voice echoed through the barrack.

"**Give them hell**, Jadwiga," the man said. "We'll finish another time."

"Wait for me, Stanek," she pleaded, but he was already out the door.

Infuriated, Jadwiga turned on the women. "How dare you, you sluts! I won't **stand for it**."

Before anyone realized what she was about to do, she bashed the two quarreling inmates' heads together. **The act was so chilling** that many of us screamed in horror.

Give them hell Punish them
stand for it accept this behavior
The act was so chilling What she did was so cruel

"Get them out of my sight," Jadwiga shouted. "Out! Out!"

From that night on I behaved like **a sleepwalker**. Everything I did was done mechanically. The consequences of the argument between the two women had caused me to shut out all emotions.

I stayed that way for days, till late one afternoon, just as the sun was about to set, I heard shots coming from a nearby hill. At first I thought the shots were directed at us—the workers with whom I was clearing the area of stones and debris. In a strange way I felt relieved that **it would soon be all over for me**. But I was wrong.

Amon Goeth, pushing his fat, burly body up the hill, held a pistol in each hand, shooting wildly into a group of people ahead of him. The women were dressed in coats and hats. They had to be new arrivals. No one in Plaszow dressed like that.

Our overseer saw how deeply the shooting affected me. I stood there with my body shaking, unable to stop. To let me know that in some way *he* was in control of **my destiny**, he called out, "You there! You are not working fast enough. If you need a rest, go up that hill. Commandant Goeth is waiting for you."

Somehow I made it through the rest of the day.

One evening many days later, while **loitering** near the barbed-wire fence, I saw Dick on the men's side. He looked much better than the last time I had seen him.

"I am so happy you survived the last inspection," I said.

....

a sleepwalker I was not awake and had no feelings
it would soon be all over for me I would die soon
my destiny what happened to me
loitering waiting, standing

"I worried a lot."

"I am better now," he said. "And I have great news."

"Tell me quickly." I was anxious to hear what the good news might be.

"The last time I saw you, I started to tell you about a man named Schindler who is taking people out of here." Dick motioned me to come closer. He didn't want others to hear what he had to say.

"This man operates a factory outside the camp. Many Jews work for him—they have been since they were deported here to Plaszow from Kraków. Here is the thing: In order to protect his workers from another deportation, possibly to Auschwitz, he is moving his factory to a small camp in Czechoslovakia."

"Goeth wouldn't let him do that."

"You're mistaken. This man Schindler has powerful connections that go beyond Amon Goeth. He **is determined** to do this. He has even **drawn up** a list of people to go to this camp."

"But why are you telling me this? This list is not going to help us."

I had not seen him so **animated** in a long time. He even smiled. "Untersturmführer Liebholt will be the commandant of this Czech camp. He insisted that fifty of the Polish prisoners of war here be included. And he also named three women. One of the women is your friend Eva."

"She got on that list?" I said with a **slight twinge** in my

....

is determined really wants
drawn up made, created
animated excited, lively
slight twinge little bit of jealousy

voice. "And you, are you one of the fifty prisoners of war?" I was on the verge of tears. Not that I wasn't happy for Dick and Eva, but I would be left alone in this awful place.

He nodded. "Guess who else is going?"

I was impatient now and somewhat envious.

"Liebholt asked for you by name!" It **came out like a bombshell**.

"He asked for me by name? How could that be?" I exclaimed. "I worked for him and his mistress in Wieliczka. **It didn't work out too well.** Liebholt was ready to throw me out a window."

"I can only tell you what I heard. Your name, Eva's, and mine are on a list of people that has been drawn up. There is one man who controls this **so-called list**. At the moment he is one of the most powerful prisoners. People are trying to **buy their way** on it."

"What if he tries to sell our places? Who could stop him from doing that?'

"Don't forget it is Liebholt who asked for us. Who would challenge him?"

I still could not comprehend why this man Schindler was going through so much trouble to save eleven hundred prisoners. Dick tried to explain that it had started out as a business and that the Jews he was now trying to save had made him rich. He saw how decent and loyal they are and how the Nazis would destroy them if he didn't do something

....

came out like a bombshell was a big shock
It didn't work out too well. They did not like me.
so-called list list our names are said to be on
buy their way pay money to get their names

to help them.

Could this be true? I wondered. I dared not raise my hopes.

I ran to find Eva so I could tell her the news. She was stunned.

"I told you that I worked for him and his mistress in Budzyn. I know he likes German-speaking servants in his house, and I **got on rather well** with Fräulein Liselotte because she loved the way I brewed coffee. But I never thought he would help me in any way. Oh, Hannelore, isn't this wonderful?"

I agreed that the news was unbelievable, but I confided to Eva that I'd had a very different experience in the Liebholt household.

....

got on rather well had a good relationship

280.		3	...ner Maria	20.12.21
281.	"	4	Wohlfeiler Chaja	4. 5.97
282.	"	5	Wohlfeiler Eugenia	18. 9.26
283.	"	6	Wohlfeiler Halina	3. 1.26
284.	"	7	Wohlfeiler Rena	29. 1.27
285.	"	8	Wohlfeiler Krystyne	9. 5.28
286.	"	9	Wohlfeiler Rosa	7. 7.03
287.	JU.Bt.	76490	Wolf Hannelore	16.10.23
288.	JU-rb.	1	Worta... Dora	20. 3.07
289.	"	2	...ken Chaja	16.12.13
290.	"	3	Zimmerowitz Elsa	18.12.13
291.	"	4	...graplta Jetti	18. 7.00
292.	"	5	Goldan ...	29. 1.18
293.	"	6	Zucker Fela	30.11.18
294.	"	7	Zuckermann Jet.l	...11...

383.	"	69230	Jakubowicz Dawid	15. 4.20
384.	"	1	Sommer Josef	21.12.14
385.	"	2	Smolarz Szymon	15. 5.04
386.	"	3	Reshen Ryszard	30. 5.21
387.	"	4	Szlamowicz Chaim	16. 5.24
388.	"	5	Kleinberg Szaja	1. 4.20
389.	"	6	Miedzibuch Michael	3.11.16
390.	"	7	Hillmann Bernard	24.12.15
391.	"	8	Königl Marek	2.11.11
392.	"	9	Jakubowicz Chaim	10. 1.19
393.	"	69240	Domb Izrael	23. 1.08
394.	"	1	Klimburt Abram	1.11.13
395.	"	2	Wisniak Abram	30
396.	"	3	Schreiber Leopold	15.10.25
397.	"	4	Silberstein Jakob	1. 1.00

Hannelore (top) and Dick (bottom) on Schindler's list.

chapter twenty

Lice became our newest enemy. They crawled around in the straw-covered bunks, and escaping them was impossible. Almost all of us had lice in our hair, clothes, and body crevices.

But something far more dangerous than lice invaded the camp too: scarlet fever. I **succumbed to** the disease shortly after it **broke out**. In spite of feeling sluggish and feverish I continued to go to work. My condition didn't escape the overseer. **There was no point in telling** him I was ill or in asking him to please understand why I couldn't work faster. He was only interested in showing the SS guard how tough he was on the prisoners.

"You are not working fast enough," he shouted at me.

He was about to use his club when Eva stepped in front of me. "Leave her alone. Can't you see she is sick?"

Eva had put herself in danger defending me. The overseer

....

Lice Little insects
succumbed to got sick from
broke out began to make other people sick
There was no point in telling It would not help me to tell

could have hit her, even clubbed her to death. I was deeply touched by her courageous act. Despite the harshness of our lives there was still goodness in people.

Toward the end of the day I was barely able to walk. After the prisoner count was done, I was unable to stand in line for the precious piece of bread. I crawled up to my bunk **in a feverish and delirious state** and spoke words no one could understand. The women asked me repeatedly to be quiet, but I was unable to stop **my rantings**.

When the morning whistle sounded, I could not lift myself. I remained on my bunk, The *Blockälteste* discovered me soon enough on her rounds through the barrack.

"Why aren't you at the place of assembly?" she screamed.

"I can't . . . get up," I replied. "I am sick."

"That's what they all say. It's laziness, if you ask me."

Barely able to lift up my head, I looked into the woman's cold eyes and said, "I . . . am . . . sick!"

"By God, you are," she shrieked. "You have red spots all over your face. It's scarlet fever! Get out at once! You're **contaminating** my barrack."

Even in my weakened state I had enough sense to leave before the *Blockälteste* reported me. Shuffling across the barrack, I fled in the direction of the infirmary, stopping every time I felt **a dizzy spell coming on**.

"Dr. Mosbach," I pleaded once inside. "Tell Dr. Mosbach it's Hannelore. I am sick."

<hr>

in a feverish and delirious state feeling very sick
my rantings the strange way I was talking
contaminating spreading your disease to
a dizzy spell coming on too sick to walk

"She is crawling with lice," the attendant said to a coworker. "Let's get her clothes off and burn them."

Without protest I let the attendants drag me to the shower. The water **lulled me into unconsciousness**. Afterward I had no idea how I'd gotten from the shower into the ward, but I did hear Dr. Mosbach's voice: "Hannelore, you have scarlet fever."

The next days were spent **in a state of semiconsciousness**, and I was not aware that SS men accompanied Dr. Mosbach on his rounds. After I regained consciousness, he made me understand how urgent it was for me to get out of the infirmary.

"They asked many questions," he said. "Only after I assured them you're going back to work did they lose interest. But the truth is you're far from being well and should not be going back to work so soon. I have to choose between the dangers, so I am sending you to the barrack of a *Blockälteste* I've come to know. She'll give you light duties. But before we release you, we will have to drain your left ear. It's infected."

Later that same day SS officers entered the infirmary. Patients were pulled from their beds. Barely able to walk, they offered no resistance. All I could hear between the shouts of the SS men was wailing and weeping. I **looked on in disbelief** and realized how close I had come to sharing the same fate had Dr. Mosbach not assured them I was going back to work.

The next afternoon one of the SS men came back to the hospital. Knowing that the SS must not find me here, Dr. Mosbach instructed Hyman, an orderly, to stuff me into the

....

lulled me into unconsciousness put me to sleep
in a state of semiconsciousness mostly sleeping
looked on in disbelief could not believe what I saw

nearest closet. It was hot inside; nonetheless, I pulled the bedsheet tighter around myself. Something in Hyman's eyes concerned me. The night before, when he had drained my ear as Dr. Mosbach had instructed him, he had that same look in his eyes. He told me how pretty I was and put his hands under the covers. I caught him in time and told him if he ever did that again, I would tell the doctor.

I must have **blacked out** from the heat in the closet, for when I **came to**, I was still in there, with Hyman standing over me, fondling my breast. "Stop!" I cried. "Stop immediately." He gave my breast one last squeeze before letting me out.

Knowing I had to leave at once, I dressed myself in the clothes Hyman had thrown on my bed.

Dr. Mosbach told me that arrangements had been made. I was to stay in barrack eight **for the time being**. The *Blockälteste* knew what to do. "Go quickly," Dr. Mosbach said.

I touched the sleeve of his white coat. "I owe you my life."

When I arrived at barrack eight, a woman came out from behind the curtained-off cubicle at the entrance. "Are you the one the doctor sent?" I nodded.

"Keep out of sight as much as possible. If a *Kapo* or SS man comes in, pretend you are cleaning."

I moved to the rear of the barrack, where I found a footstool to sit on. I fell asleep almost immediately. Someone tapping my shoulder woke me up. The *Blockälteste* stood over me holding a small enamel pot. "This is for you. The doctor's wife

....

blacked out fainted
came to woke up
for the time being until I was better

sent it. Go on, eat. **Get some meat on your bones.** You look like a *Musselman!*"

Nothing had ever tasted so good, and I scraped the pot until there wasn't **a morsel** of food left.

The women returned from work in the late afternoon, and the barrack **came alive** with chatter. To my surprise Eva was among them. I knew barrack eight was where she lived, but in my fatigued state I must have forgotten. I didn't let Eva hug or kiss me for fear I might still be contagious, yet it was obvious how happy we were to see each other.

"Thank God you're alive," she said. "The infirmary is a dangerous place."

When it was time to go to the place of assembly, the *Blockälteste* held me back. "You stay here."

I again retreated to my little footstool and daydreamed about Dick. Did he know I had been in the infirmary? Was he still in Plaszow? If only Fella were still with me . . . she would know what to do.

It was very quiet in the barrack, so when I thought I heard some movement coming from one of the upper bunks. I turned. But no one was there. Moments later the rustling of straw caught my attention. A board was being lifted, and a small hand emerged first. Then the head of a little girl popped up for just a moment. Before I could get another look, the board went down again. I understood what was happening. Someone had **devised** a hiding place underneath a bunk to keep a child alive.

....

Get some meat on your bones. Gain some weight.
a morsel the smallest piece
came alive was filled
devised built, made

Later, when the women returned from the head count, I watched a young woman go over to the place where the board had been lifted. I was certain she was the mother of this child.

During the night I heard the usual outbursts: "Take your feet away . . . I can't breathe. . . . Get away from me." I was used to it and usually went right back to sleep. Not this night. So many thoughts went through my mind. Where was Dick? Was it really true—that there was a list of people who would be able to leave Plaszow?

"I don't believe Oskar Schindler will get us out of here," Eva said the next day. "The group of women who have been working for him for some time swear it's true, but it seems impossible to me."

"Dick believes it," I said.

No one had seen Dick. Even Eva couldn't find out where he might be.

When I felt stronger and there was new talk of transports leaving Plaszow, I went back to my own barrack. Some of the women who worked for Schindler were now there. They **regarded me as an outsider** because I hadn't been working among them in Schindler's factory. So all my inquiries about where the Schindler men were **fell on deaf ears**. Part of it was because **of the language barrier**. I didn't speak Polish, and only a few of the women spoke German. But by now I understood some Yiddish, a universal language among most Jews. I believed the women **resented my being** on the list.

....

regarded me as an outsider saw me as a stranger
fell on deaf ears did not get answered
of the language barrier I did not speak their language
resented my being were angry because I was

They would have rather had one of their friends or relatives take my place.

I went to the barbed-wire fence as often as I could and called across to the men's side to see if anyone knew a man named Hillman. No one had seen him. I feared he had already left.

One time, when I was trying to find out about Dick, I heard a scream. It took only a second to realize that a man had **flung** himself onto the electrified fence to end his life. His body twitched, and then the hissing of burned flesh filled the air. Through tears I recited the Kaddish, the prayer for the dead.

During the following weeks many transports left Plaszow. Inmates spoke in whispers about camps called Auschwitz, Mauthausen, Gross-Rosen, and Bergen-Belsen—names I was not familiar with, yet I was filled with fear of ending up in one of them rather than the one promised. But the so-called Schindler women still seemed **optimistic**.

....

flung thrown
optimistic hopeful and believed the list was real

BEFORE YOU MOVE ON...

1. **Problem and Solution** How was being on Schindler's list a solution for some of the Jewish prisoners?

2. **Summarize** Reread pages 152–158. What were some obstacles that the prisoners faced every day?

LOOK AHEAD Read pages 159–176 to find out what kept Hannelore alive.

chapter twenty-one

The quiet of the night was interrupted by the sound of boots and barking dogs. The door to my barrack was yanked open by SS men shouting orders. One of them proceeded to read names off a list, names of the Schindler women, the ones who worked for this man. And then my name was being called: Hannelore Wolff. Two hundred ninety-seven women had worked for Oskar Schindler in his factory right outside Plaszow. Now three more names were being included among them, the three that Untersturmführer Liebholt had requested.

Shouts of joy filled the barrack. "We are going to Oskar Schindler's camp!"

I too **got caught up in the excitement of the moment**. I grabbed my meager possessions, a metal soup bowl and wooden spoon, and followed the others walking toward waiting cattle cars. Eva joined me. She had been brought over from

....

got caught up in the excitement of the moment became excited because we were leaving barrack eight with more of the Schindler women. I grabbed her hand, squeezing it hard. "Eva, now I believe it. We are going to Oskar Schindler's camp."

Even when the iron bar was placed across the door of the cattle car, it was not as traumatic as it had been on previous journeys, nor were the crowded conditions inside as horribly bad. After all, we were going to a place where life would be better.

The train was going fast, and when it came to a curve, we fell over one another. Normally there would have been **outcries**. Not now, **for the atmosphere was one of hope**. Soon the women began to sing Polish songs of freedom and love, none of which I understood. But I caught the excitement and hummed. After many hours without food or water we all grew weary. Added to our discomfort was the stench from a pail used as a toilet. It had overflowed. The stench became unbearable.

By now I was so hungry that I started to eat a small piece of bread I had saved. I felt guilty eating it, knowing all eyes were on me. But it wasn't only hunger that nagged at us; our thirst was unrelenting, too. We started to fight among ourselves. Too much room for one person, too little for another. Standing near a crack in the wall was a prize—one could get some air to breathe.

After agonizing days and nights of **rattling and jousting**, the train came to a halt. All of us breathed a sigh of relief. We had been pressed against one another for too long, and now it

....

outcries shouting, yelling

for the atmosphere was one of hope because people finally had hope that they would live

rattling and jousting the train moving and people pushing against each other would finally end. Strangely enough, the doors remained shut. Day turned to evening; darkness fell. Not a sound could be heard from the outside.

A woman, **seemingly in a trance, looked in my direction, almost hypnotizing me**. Then her arms went up in a helpless sort of way, and her bloodless lips seized air in whistling gasps. At first I didn't understand what was happening, but when the sounds stopped and the woman **slumped** over, I knew. Now the odor of death invaded the cattle car.

Suddenly dogs barked. Heavy footsteps fell alongside the train. Someone lifted the iron bar and the door opened. We knew without being told that this was not Brünnlitz, where Schindler had established his new factory. The usual orders to get out sounded harsher, more urgent. At a signal a group of men wearing striped pants and jackets with caps to match climbed aboard and began shoving us off the train. They looked grotesque in uniforms that didn't fit. They did nothing on their own, moving only at the command of their leader, who cried, "Faster, faster!"

"Where are we?" I asked one of the men.

"Auschwitz," he whispered back.

Auschwitz! That place had been described to me as the **worst hellhole** on Earth. I shivered with fright, not knowing what awaited us. SS men dressed in heavy overcoats guarded us, but for us prisoners, standing in our thin dresses, there

....

seemingly in a trance, looked in my direction, almost hypnotizing me who looked like she was dreaming, stared at me and I could not look away

slumped fell, leaned

worst hellhole most terrible place

was no protection from the harsh November night and the howling winds. I remembered my warm winter coat, the one I wore when leaving Weimar. How I wished I had it now. I still remembered Mama's argument when I had wanted to take my good navy coat—the one I loved so much.

"Hannelore, be practical," she'd said. "The loden coat is warmer; it will serve you better."

My anxiety increased minute by minute. Where were we? Then I heard music. An orchestra of men in striped uniforms was playing **a lively waltz** that would normally have **enchanted me**, but here in this grim place the music sounded bizarre.

Our transport had not arrived alone. Along the way from Plaszow many cars had been added to the train. We had heard lots of commotion but couldn't see anything. Cattle cars had no windows. Now, with people of all ages and in all conditions getting out, one car at a time, the SS men and women looked at us all with **contempt**. I shrank into nothingness, hoping not to be noticed lest the truncheons they held up in the air would come down on me.

Two cars away an SS man in a black uniform and white gloves was waving a whip left and right at the men and women who had just **disembarked**.

The line to the left soon swelled with elderly people and small children crying and wailing. A girl walking alongside me whispered what being in the left line meant: "They will die before this night is over."

....

a lively waltz upbeat music
enchanted me made me happy
contempt hatred, disgust
disembarked gotten off the train

Where was Eva? Being so very frightened, I didn't realize that I had lost sight of her. I dared not look back for fear the SS woman walking alongside us would use her **spiked club** on me.

Would the SS men see that there had been a mistake? That we didn't belong in Auschwitz? Would we three hundred women be loaded back on the train to go to **our real destination**?

When a girl from our group walking next to me saw my tears, she was emphatic. "Save your tears," she said. "You are on Oskar Schindler's list. You have nothing to worry about. He will get us out of here!"

"I wish I could believe it," I sobbed out. "How can he get anyone out of *this* place?"

I looked for Eva, hoping she would assure me a mistake had been made in sending us here. Eva was nowhere in sight.

★ ★ ★

It was daybreak, but the sun wasn't visible and the few tufts of grass in sight were covered with silvery frost. There seemed to be no end to the marching. My thin legs buckled under me, and I didn't know how much longer I could go on walking. At last we arrived at a gate.

The women talked in hushed voices, assuring one another that Oskar Schindler would **come to our rescue**. But until then it would be difficult to stay alive. This place held no promises.

....

spiked club stick that had pieces of metal on it
our real destination Schindler's camp
come to our rescue save us

Naively, I wanted to tell my captors about their mistake: We were needed for important work in Oskar Schindler's camp. If only I could tell them now before stepping through the gate. But afraid of being beaten for **speaking up**, I just walked through the portal, praying to God to help me.

Along the way a group of prisoners dressed in coarse, striped trousers held up by ropes were sweeping the road. Unshaven, **gaunt, shrunken**, they barely resembled human beings. One man had no cap. His closely shaven head gave him the appearance of an ape.

I started trembling and couldn't stop. The thought that there had been a time when these men were normal human beings, with families, **completely unnerved me**. One of the men pushed a wheelbarrow. He came closer. In a thin, lifeless voice he pleaded, "Give me your food."

How I wished I had something to give! But I had nothing.

I trudged on, terrified. The sight of the prisoners, the high barbed-wire fences, the watchtowers . . . it all seemed hopeless. The wind shifted, and smoke coming from a chimney surrounded us.

"That is a lot of smoke," I said.

"Burning flesh," the girl walking alongside me explained. "Can't you smell it?" She felt compelled to give me details. "You'll see. They will order us to take a shower, but it's not a real shower. There are no drains in the floor. What comes through the showerheads is gas."

....

Naively Innocently, Ignorantly
speaking up saying something to a guard
gaunt, shrunken very skinny and sick looking
completely unnerved me made me feel sick

I listened in disbelief.

"When everyone is dead, the bodies are put in a **crematorium**, like that one, to burn."

"You are **out of your mind**," I snapped. But I had to admit the odor did seem to be that of burned flesh. Could the girl be telling the truth?

When it was my turn to enter the shower chamber, I was convinced my end had come. Concealing a creased picture of my family in the palm of my hand (I wanted to look at their faces before my life **was snuffed out**), I entered the shower room. Uniformed SS guards hurried us on, making vulgar remarks, pressing us against one another. As the door bolted from the outside we cried and whimpered. Some people prayed: "Hear, O Israel, the Lord our God, the Lord is One." I would have liked to join in the prayer, but the words wouldn't come. I felt as if I had died already.

Minutes passed. Still nothing came through the showerheads, not even a **fine mist**. I wanted it to go faster.

"God, if I must die, make it fast," I cried.

And then, as if my prayers had been answered, something started coming out of the showerheads, only it wasn't gas, it was . . . *water!* I hugged a complete stranger. Both of us laughed and cried at the same time.

It was then that I spotted Eva. Thank God she was alive. We hugged and kissed. Words were not necessary. Together we ran naked and wet through the cold night to the next barrack

....

crematorium large furnace; fire
out of your mind insane, crazy
was snuffed out ended
fine mist little bit of water

where the smell of chemicals was so strong, it made me dizzy and nauseous. A barber, a prisoner in a striped uniform, worked with great speed cutting my hair right down to my scalp. When the **dull clippers grazed** my skin again and again, I flinched. But he was stronger and rougher; there was no way to escape his grip. I was passed on to another barber who shaved off my pubic hair while I stood on a stool before him. The razor cut into my flesh, sending a stream of blood down my legs. Then I was sprayed with a burning, evil-smelling substance that **reeked of carbolic acid**.

Out in the cold again to the next barrack, where a striped dress, something that resembled underwear, a torn piece of fabric for my bald head, and wooden clogs were thrown at me. I pulled the dress over my head, put on the stained panties, and tied the kerchief around my head, fastening it under my chin.

Thousands of female prisoners milled around with nowhere to go. No one spoke. Only SS men could be heard shouting orders.

I'd had nothing to eat but a piece of bread since leaving Plaszow, and the only drink had come from the showerheads. I thought of Papa and how much he must have suffered in Buchenwald. Papa had lasted only six weeks. I wondered how long it would take me to succumb in this evil place.

My hunger was so intense, I **started to lose touch with reality**. I dreamt of Dick and our happy **stolen** moments. Was he safe in Schindler's camp? Or had he, too, been betrayed

....

dull clippers grazed razor touched
reeked of carbolic acid smelled like chemicals
started to lose touch with reality could not think
stolen secret

and ended up elsewhere? The plans we'd made together, the planting of a lilac tree like the one at home . . . those dreams were all that **sustained me** now.

We were herded into a windowless hut with a wet, muddy floor. I found a bunk near Hella, one of the Schindler women. Hella had been among the privileged prisoners in Plaszow. Her older brothers found ways to get extra food to her. Now she sat alone, sobbing.

"Hella, why are you crying? Didn't you tell me this morning that your Oskar Schindler will get us out of here?" I asked.

"That was before I knew we were in Birkenau. **What good can he do** us now? We'll all **go up in smoke**! If only they had let us stay in Auschwitz, we could have worked awhile. And who knows—by then the war might be over. But here in Birkenau there is no chance."

Birkenau, I came to learn, was where **the exterminations took place**. It was a part of Auschwitz.

I found Eva in one of the last rows of bunks. She looked pale, and she was shivering in her thin dress. "This is the end," she said, crying softly into her hands. "Do you think it was all a hoax from the beginning?'

"I don't know anything anymore," I said, crying along with her.

While standing at attention at the place of assembly that night, I turned my head to the left, where I presumed the crematorium stood. The sun had set directly behind the brick

....

sustained me gave me strength
What good can he do How can he help
go up in smoke be killed and burned
the exterminations took place people were killed

building, outlining it in silhouette. The trees were laden with ashes. It could have been a beautiful autumn scene, but I knew only too well what lay behind that beauty.

The camp lights cast their powerful beams everywhere; even the barbed-wire fence began to glow. Prisoners streamed out of the barracks, filling the giant square, where talk was not permitted. A fine drizzle soon saturated my thin dress and seeped into my clogs. There was nothing I could do but stand **rooted to** the ground till the assembly was dismissed. I **envied the SS women their** warm capes and gloves, their well-fed bodies untouched by cold and rain. I took care not to draw attention to myself. The leather thongs they carried had sharp iron tips.

At last the count began. Thousands of women lined the square, all resembling one another in a nameless, faceless way. I saw myself in them. The thought of ending my own life crossed my mind.

It rained continually for the next week, and all I would have had to do was let myself sink into the mud. A *Kapo* would do the rest. He would thrash me with his club until there was no trace of life left. In my mind I **took leave of** all the people I had loved in life. Only when it came to saying good-bye to Dick did I hesitate. Had we not promised each other not to give up, no matter what happened?

And so I struggled on. Every night I prayed, asking God to give me the will to get through another day and not to

....

rooted to very still on
envied the SS women their was jealous that the SS women wore
took leave of said good-bye to

succumb to despair. Staying alive in Birkenau would take an unbelievable effort.

I retreated into my **dreamworld** more and more often now, especially when there was trouble and the numbers at the place of assembly didn't add up. One of my most comforting dreams had to do with food. In my dream the street was flooded with glorious sunshine. Well-dressed men and women strolled leisurely down the street. Now and then someone stopped to say "Good day," but I never recognized anyone. I just kept on walking down a narrow street following the **aroma** of freshly baked bread.

Suddenly something quite wonderful happened. I found myself standing in front of a bakery. My eyes opened wide when I saw the display of crusty rolls and breads. Automatically, I pushed the brass handle on the framed glass door and entered.

"Good morning," the woman behind the counter said. "We have fresh raisin rolls today. How many would you like?"

"I'll take three, please," I answered, wondering how the salesperson knew raisin rolls were my favorite.

The shout of "Dismissed!" **brought me back to reality, transforming** me again into a prisoner at Auschwitz-Birkenau.

....

dreamworld memories and thoughts

aroma smell, odor

brought me back to reality, transforming woke me up from my dream, changing

chapter twenty-two

Snowflakes clung to my eyelids, eyebrows, even my lips. In some ways it was a blessing, for the snowflakes relieved my thirst and filled my stomach, just a little. But a constant chill extended up from my feet and **gnawed at my insides**. My dress and wooden clogs were always **damp**. They never had a chance to dry out.

Aside from food, uninterrupted sleep was what I longed for most. But the clattering of trains arriving in the middle of the night made that impossible. The new arrivals who assembled in the camp's square looked as bewildered as I had been on my first day. Some carried knapsacks, while others just stood there **empty-handed**. *What fine clothes they have on,* I marveled. *Before **day's end** they, too, will be in gray clothes; they, too, will have nothing else.* When asked how long I had been here, I could give only a vague answer. To me it seemed like months, but it might

---

gnawed at my insides made me cold everywhere
damp a little wet
empty-handed holding nothing
day's end the end of the day

have been only a few weeks. Since I worked only occasionally, cleaning out barracks or sweeping the streets, time didn't go by very fast.

The windowless hut I lived in was nothing more than **a bunch of boards hastily** nailed together. The icy winds seeped through the cracks, making it as cold inside as it was outside. The thin, **lice-infested blankets** offered little warmth. And no matter how often I picked lice off my head and clothes, they always came back, sucking my blood, giving me no rest.

Then there was Hella, complaining through most of the night.

"Your feet are in my mouth, imbecile. You are taking up too much room on my part of the bunk." Her complaints were never-ending.

During the day Hella set herself apart from the others by walking alone, seldom talking to anyone, and acting as though she were too good, too noble, to **associate with** the women in the barrack.

I spent most of my time on Eva's bunk. My friend had withdrawn into her own world. She sat mumbling to herself, picking lice. Eva worried me.

The older women sat on their bunks talking of food and recipes. It helped pass the time till the cauldron with the noon soup arrived. Then everyone scrambled down from the bunks for fear of **being left out**.

It was the same for me. I didn't care if my hands were

....

a bunch of boards hastily pieces of wood quickly
lice-infested blankets blankets covered with bugs
associate with talk to or be friends with
being left out not getting any food

dirty or if the blood from picking off lice was still under my fingernails. All I worried about was if the ladle would go deep enough to come up with a turnip or a piece of potato peel for me. Then my worries increased when the pain in my back and abdomen returned as time went on. This made standing for hours at the place of assembly more difficult.

Our *Blockälteste* was neither gentle nor kind. I was therefore surprised to hear a softer tone of voice when she made an announcement: "I need ten volunteers this morning for a blood test. It doesn't hurt, and you'll get a cup of milk afterward."

It was hard to resist a cup of milk. I was about to raise my hand when I remembered something Fella had said when we first met: "Don't *ever* volunteer. It's never anything that will benefit you. I did it once. They made me clean barracks all night long. I still had to go to work in the morning. It wasn't worth the little extra food they gave me that day."

Still, I longed for that cup of milk. I could almost taste it.

The ten women who did volunteer didn't return for several days. When they came back, **there was talk of sterilization, of being robbed of their womanhood**.

Apart from being fed, the most important part of the day for us occurred in the evening: **going to the latrine**. The open toilet with twelve holes cut out of a board was a privilege for which permission was needed. One night I was lucky. I made it in before the curfew whistle sounded, with time to spare to use the washroom. The absence of soap and a towel was no longer

....

there was talk of sterilization, of being robbed of their womanhood people said these women had operations so that they could not have babies

going to the latrine using the toilet and shower

an issue. Such luxuries did not exist in Birkenau. I used the hem of my dress to dry myself.

The three hundred women who were on Oskar Schindler's list for Brünnlitz had thus far been untouched by the dreaded selections. But then came the morning when SS women moved us to a hut closer to the shower barrack. Huddled on my new bunk, I tried to **make peace with** my fate, for I knew moving could mean only one thing.

Then I walked over to Eva's bunk. I was glad to see her eyes didn't **have that vacant look**. No longer silent, as she had been ever since we arrived in Birkenau, she started talking. "No matter what happens, we'll be friends to the end," she said.

We hugged and we cried, thinking **our days were numbered**.

When I heard children walking by the hut, whimpering and crying out for their mothers, I felt as if my heart were breaking apart. I rushed to the door wanting to offer a kind word. Unable to get nearer to them as they clutched their dolls and teddy bears, I listened as SS men **spurred them on** to walk faster, telling them they would see their mothers sooner if they did. I knew only too well where they were headed.

Later that night sickening fumes from the crematorium filled the hut.

New transports arrived daily, bringing Jews from Hungary and

....

make peace with accept
have that vacant look look like she was dead
our days were numbered we would die soon
spurred them on told them

Greece who told tales of mass deportations throughout Europe. One day Birkenau was **brimming with** people; the next day it was nearly empty. I wondered why I was being kept alive.

Winter had come, this much I knew, for it was very cold. Though what year it was no longer was clear. Hunger and **sleep deprivation had wreaked havoc on** my memory. Night after night I woke up in a cold sweat expecting it to be my turn for the gas chamber.

One afternoon I had diarrhea and was given special permission to use the toilet. When I returned, the entrance to the barrack was blocked by SS men. I tried running because I feared this meant selection. A guard saw what I was doing and pulled me back.

"This pig here tried running away!" he shouted.

I had been through selections before, but this one was far more serious. An SS man pointed left or right while his assistant entered names or numbers into a ledger. Quickly, I undressed while waiting in line. I pinched my cheeks to make them look **rosy**.

The SS man conducting the selections pointed to the left when it was my turn. My hands began to tremble; my back stiffened into a cramp. I wanted to scream but let out a barely audible groan. Dazed, I dressed and waited to be led outside. Guards had their rifles on me as well as on other prisoners in this line, as if we had the strength to resist our death sentence.

The sun's orange glow merged with the smoke coming from

....

brimming with full of
sleep deprivation had wreaked havoc on being unable to
sleep had destroyed
rosy healthy

the crematorium, creating a most unusual sight. It was as though the sun had been caught in a net of smoke. This was a sunset like I had never seen before. *My last sunset*, I thought: *I will never see another.* Soon they would come for me, tell me the lie that I was to take a shower—one with gas.

While waiting for **the inevitable**, I watched as other prisoners marched in rows of five, singing a popular camp song. They seemed to be strong and vigorous. That was the odd thing about Auschwitz-Birkenau: **contradictions, contradictions**. *They must work in the crematorium, getting extra rations*, I thought. That's why they looked so well fed.

The refrain of their song was always the same: "Never say this is your last walk." I had heard the song before; I could hum it. However, this time it sounded as if the refrain was meant for me.

Soon another group of prisoners marched by, and while the guards were looking elsewhere, I slipped into **the quickening flow of these** marchers. If the women in this group saw what I had done, they did not betray me. I worked alongside them that evening, carrying stones from one place to another, not quite clear why. It was exhausting. It would soon be time for the nightly roll call, and that worried me. I had no choice but to march to the place of assembly.

Blockältestes walked back and forth, consulting lists. There was something wrong with the count. "I have one too many," I heard my *Blockälteste* say.

---

the inevitable what was going to happen

contradictions, contradictions many things did not make sense

the quickening flow of these this group of

It took hours to tally the numbers. In the end we were dismissed. I went back to my barrack as if I still belonged. When Eva saw me, she came running with **outstretched** arms. "Hannelore, thank God you are here. How did you do it?"

When the *Blockälteste* saw us, she cried out, "It was you who **held up** the count! I should **turn you in**."

I **shrugged my shoulders** and walked away.

"It will cost you. You better be prepared to pay," the *Blockälteste* shouted after me. But I already knew that I would have to part with my bread ration.

It was a small price to pay for my life.

....

outstretched open
held up caused problems with
turn you in tell the guards about you
shrugged my shoulders showed that I did not care

BEFORE YOU MOVE ON...

1. **Conclusions** Reread page 168. Hannelore thought about ending her own life. What stopped her?

2. **Comparisons** Reread pages 164–169. How was Auschwitz-Birkenau worse than other concentration camps?

LOOK AHEAD Read pages 177–188 to learn how Hannelore saved a prisoner.

chapter twenty-three

In time my hair grew back. It wasn't as though I had a full head of hair again, but a little bit of stubble began to grow and there were even a few curls. Every time my hand went up to touch the curls, I smiled. Having hair would make me look and feel like a girl again.

There was little else to smile about. Although I was always hungry, it was impossible to eat the watery soup because it tasted funny, like it was **laced** with chemicals. And it smelled bad, too. Hella thought the chemicals were put into the soup to stop our menstrual periods.

Winter wouldn't end that year. Sleet and freezing rain fell on top of the **packed** snow. Except for going to the place of assembly, we stayed inside the hut, where **infectious diseases ran rampant**. One day I developed a bad head cold. Earlier I had looked through a pile of garbage, hoping to find some

....

laced mixed
packed piles of
infectious diseases ran rampant illnesses were spreading quickly and making everyone sick

potato peels I could eat, but I saw nothing except some rags, **frayed strips** from a torn blanket. I wrapped the rags around my head, making the icy-cold barrack just a little more tolerable.

Another day I found a **shard** of mirror in Hella's bunk. Unable to resist, I took a look at myself. What I saw was a skeleton whose wrinkled skin resembled that of an old woman.

Oh God, I thought, *if this is what I have become, they are certain to take me away with the next selection.* I waited for it to happen.

Miraculously, Eva felt better again, but the endless cold days lingered like a dark curtain. The older women continued to huddle together, exchanging recipes, reminiscing about the past. Oskar Schindler's name was seldom mentioned anymore.

My suffering continued. Night after night I **was wracked with** pain in my back and belly. My skeleton-like body rubbed against the planks of the bunk. There was no comfort to be had except in my dreams. I **made ample use of them**—the only escape available to me.

One night in a dream I imagined I heard someone shouting, "Schindler women, up and out!"

What a delightful dream, I thought, rubbing my eyes. To my astonishment I realized it was not a dream at all. Several SS men were standing in the center of the hut reading off names, not numbers. I heard Eva's name being called loud and clear: "Eva Suesskind." This was unbelievable! How could it be? Anxiously, I waited for my own name to be called. At last I heard it: "Hannelore Wolff."

....

frayed strips ripped pieces
shard piece
was wracked with felt a lot of
made ample use of them dreamed a lot

I rushed down from my bunk to **catch up with** Eva. There was music playing as we marched outside. I recognized the lively tune of "Rosamunde." It was too good to be true; we had been addressed as "Schindler women"!

Overseers with yellow patches sewn to their striped uniforms, identifying them as Jews, hurried us on. There was no time for sluggishness. No words were exchanged. I tried hard to **keep up the pace**, but suddenly I stopped. The rosy reflections of the early dawn outlined an unmoving shape lying across the electric fence—the shape of a woman. Her right arm was raised upward as if in prayer, stretching toward the sky. Her head **dangled** backward. My body shuddered at the sight, a reminder of what I had **contemplated** many times myself.

The doors to the waiting cattle cars had been opened. The overseers worked with brutal speed, pushing us inside. One prisoner standing on the ground tugged at my dress as I went up the ramp, stopping me. He pressed a piece of paper in my hand and then spoke to me in rapid Yiddish: "You have a chance of staying alive away from this place. Please, if you do survive, contact the people whose names I have written down. Tell them you saw me in Auschwitz, at the end of 1944." Before I had a chance to tell him I would do as he asked, he was gone.

In spite of the joy at leaving Auschwitz and the promise of going to Oskar Schindler's camp, it proved to be a difficult trip for all of us. On our journey to Auschwitz we had not been as frail—we had been better able to cope with the horrid

....

catch up with walk next to
keep up the pace walk quickly with everyone else
dangled hung
contemplated thought about doing

conditions inside the crammed cattle car.

Tears came easily now. Just thinking of Dick and my family started me sobbing. I still had a few crumpled photographs of my family hidden in my clogs. I remembered every detail of those pictures; even without looking I could **conjure up** the images. There were Mama and Papa at a resort called Bad Nauheim. Mama, beautifully dressed in a steel gray outfit that hugged her small waist and flared out into a full skirt. Her hair was piled on top of her head, as had been the fashion. Papa, looking handsome, held a cane in his right hand. He stood behind Mama, one hand draped protectively around her shoulder. How **stately** they both looked! Mama had told me the picture was taken on **their honeymoon**.

Hannelore's parents, Karoline and Martin Wolff.

....

conjure up clearly see
stately handsome, elegant
their honeymoon a trip after their wedding

The other photograph was of Wolfgang and Selly, both of them smiling, their eyes **full of mischief**. That's how I remembered my brothers.

But Papa was dead and so was Selly. I would never, ever see them again. And what about Mama and Wolfgang? If only I knew for certain what had happened to them . . .

I was so caught up in **remembrances of times** past that I didn't pay attention to what was going on around me until someone grabbed my arm. "You're the only one she will talk to. Do something."

I turned and saw what all the commotion was about. Some women had tried to take a piece of bread away from Hella. Screaming at them, she guarded the chunk of bread **ferociously**. But they kept on **baiting her**.

"We don't want very much, just one bite."

"It's mine," Hella shouted. "Now get away from me!"

The women lunged at her and grabbed the piece of bread. Hella's face was ablaze. She let out a guttural sound and said, "I hope the Germans kill all of you."

"I don't want to talk to her after what she just said," I said.

A woman named Rosie, who had appointed herself our leader, was still fairly strong. Approaching Hella in a menacing way, she said, "You are one of us, whether you like it or not. If the Germans kill us, that means you will be killed, too."

Hella kept on screaming, insisting that her piece of bread be returned. Eva and I looked on in silence.

After what seemed like an endless trip, the train stopped.

....

full of mischief showing that they liked to have fun
remembrances of times my memories of the
ferociously like an animal
baiting her saying things to her to make her angry

God, let this be Brünnlitz, I prayed. *I don't know how much longer I can hold out on this stinking train. I'm so thirsty, my tongue is sticking to the roof of my mouth.*

The Nazi who opened the door had a mean look on his face. Instead of ordering us to get out fast, as was the usual command, he pointed his **riding crop** at Hella.

"You. Empty the pail," he shouted.

Hella froze. When no one else moved, I stepped forward. Not obeying the Nazi's order quickly could **have deadly consequences**.

Carrying the heavy pail was an unbelievable task. I gagged from the odor and became nauseous. Hoping **the nausea would subside** if I paused for a moment, I started to set the pail down.

"Move, you swine, or I'll make you drink it," the SS man threatened, kicking me in the shins and making the pail's contents splatter on my dress.

After I emptied the pail behind the tracks. I got back on the train, covered with waste, ashamed of my own foul smell. All eyes were on me. Before long the train began to move again.

"Look here, **this was of your own doing**," Rosie said. "He pointed at Hella, not you."

"But she didn't move," I replied. "No one moved. Who knows how it would have ended had I not stepped forward?"

Rosie relented then, ordering people to move aside and make room for me in a corner. She covered me with a blanket.

....

riding crop whip
have deadly consequences mean he would kill us
the nausea would subside I would not feel as sick
this was of your own doing you decided to carry the pail

"Rest now. You deserve it," she said.

Soon Hella knelt before me. "How you must hate me," she said. "I **couldn't bear to touch** that pail. Now you're suffering for it."

I didn't say anything to Hella, but I managed a weak smile before closing my eyes. Eva watched over me, making sure no one stepped on me. I wondered if she remembered the time she had saved me from a *Kapo*, just as I had saved Hella from the Nazi.

....

couldn't bear to touch could not tolerate emptying

chapter twenty-four

We stumbled out of the cattle cars and looked around.

The air smelled different, and the morning sun was so strong that it melted the packed snow. Ashamed of my stinking dress, I trailed behind the others.

There he was, standing at the platform, the same Untersturmführer Liebholt who had threatened to throw me out the window in Wieliczka. I had not seen him since that day, and I was still afraid of him. **But the irony of it all did not escape me.** I had been able to leave Auschwitz to come here only because he had demanded it.

There was no shouting, no barking dogs. Only a stern official ordering us to walk up the hill. Seeing that I was having a hard time keeping up with the others, Hella put her arm around my waist, and Eva trailed behind us.

....

But the irony of it all did not escape me. But I understood that even though this man scared me, he is the one who saved me.

"I am still ashamed of what I did," Hella said. "Let me **make it up to you**." It was certainly better than walking on my own, so I gratefully accepted her help.

In the distance a cluster of buildings appeared. I thought it was our camp. "Look over there. That must be Brünnlitz," I said.

Hella's face turned white. "All I see are chimneys."

"Nonsense, Hella. Smell the air. It's nothing like Birkenau. These chimneys have a different purpose. They are not what you think."

Suddenly Hella's face broke out in a smile. "Look! That man in the Tyrolean hat, that's Oskar Schindler!"

I had imagined him to be small and portly, but he wasn't. Before us stood a **dashing, charismatic figure of a** man. His voice **generated trust** as he assured us that we had nothing to worry about. Pointing to a large building, he said, "Go inside. There is soup and bread waiting for you."

The people who knew him well and had worked for him in his Kraków factory smiled at one another, as if they had known all along that he would come to their rescue. For me it was a different matter. I was too tired and sick to fully appreciate the situation. All I wanted was to rest. Not even the promise of food **tempted me**.

Once inside the small camp we heard jubilant cries coming from a balcony to the left. Many men stood there waving, calling names. As the men and women recognized one another the cries got louder.

---

make it up to you do something nice for you
dashing, charismatic figure of a handsome
generated trust made us feel safe
tempted me made me feel happy

Then, above the other voices, came *his:* "Little one, I have been looking for you all over!"

I did not look up, even when the voice called me a second time. Fear that it wasn't real made me ignore him. Besides, I was a skeleton dressed in rags, not the girl he had met in Budyzn. I **shuffled along** like a sleepwalker, letting myself be pushed up a staircase into a large, rectangular room. I found out later that our room was above the factory.

Exhausted from the journey and the excitement of the day, I was about to collapse. Eva took my arm, guiding me toward the food. "Come, we'll eat," she coaxed. "The soup smells heavenly."

Chunks of meat and vegetables were poured into my canteen. This was the best food I had eaten since leaving home. I ate, but I had difficulty keeping my thoughts straight. Had it really been Dick Hillman shouting to me from the balcony? Perhaps I had been **hallucinating**.

More than anything else, I wanted to sleep, but first I had to take a shower and find clean clothes. I moved around in the shower, making certain every part of my body was clean. I dug my fingernails into my scalp, massaging and rubbing. In the end I had to give up. I simply could not stand on my feet any longer. The clothes given to me smelled fresh, and even though they were much too big, I didn't care.

My eyes kept closing. It took great effort to stay awake while I waited for everyone to finish showering.

....

shuffled along walked slowly
hallucinating dreaming, imagining

The second contact with the men came when a letter was pushed through a loose brick in the wall. It **gave an account of** the time they had spent in the Gross-Rosen concentration camp in Austria and of their journey to Brünnlitz. Once they had arrived, Schindler promised the men he would get the women out of Auschwitz, too. Then they wrote about Liebholt, their commandant. He was overheard having said that it was his aim to destroy every living Jew. Schindler had **his hands full** controlling him.

Eva had **checked out** other things while I was resting. "Come see for yourself," she said. "We share a balcony with the men. The only thing separating us is a mesh-wire fence. The space is narrow, but that shouldn't stop us."

However, the line of women waiting to talk to their men was so great, I didn't have the strength to push forward. For now only the very determined succeeded.

Later that day someone called me to come to the balcony. Dick stood on the other side of the mesh fence looking remarkably well. His eyes again had the same glow that had first attracted me back in Budzyn. I was overcome by the joy of the moment and didn't know what to say. **Giving way to tears**, I explained that I had been ill for a long time and had not expected to ever see him again.

"We are together now," he said, trying to soothe me. "I've already found a job for you in the SS kitchen, where it is warm and where you'll have enough to eat."

....

gave an account of explained
his hands full a hard time
checked out looked around at
Giving way to tears Crying

We met every night after that, and although there could be no physical contact, it was enough to be able to see him and talk with him. Sometimes I placed my hands on the fence that separated us. He would do the same from his side.

Dick worked in the camp kitchen, so he could again bring me sweetened coffee and bread, as he'd done in Budzyn so long ago. The extra food made me stronger, and I soon felt much better.

During our time at Budzyn, Dick hadn't wanted me to know anything about his activities, afraid of putting me in **jeopardy**. But now he told me freely of his association with Czech partisans.

"Most of our food comes from the partisans now," he explained. "They also have provided us with guns, for when the time comes to use them, and a radio. The Russians are advancing with great speed. It is only a **matter of months** before the Germans will be forced to **surrender**. Our biggest obstacle is Liebholt. He has vowed to destroy every Jew." Dick's face grew serious again. "We are so close to freedom, and yet it might still go the other way."

....

jeopardy danger
matter of months short time
surrender admit they lost the war

BEFORE YOU MOVE ON...

1. **Inference** Reread pages 182–183. Hannelore carried the pail for Hella. What does this show about her?

2. **Conclusions** Reread pages 186–187. How did Hannelore's life improve at Brünnlitz?

LOOK AHEAD Read pages 189–200 to learn how Schindler helped more Jewish people.

chapter twenty-five

"Close your eyes, I have a surprise for you," Dick teased. He was in a joyous mood this evening.

"Give me a clue."

"Let's see. It was first seen in paradise."

"Paradise was at the beginning of time. I can't possibly guess what that has to do with your surprise. Tell me what it is."

"Promise to keep your eyes closed. Now put your hand over the wire."

When I discovered he had placed an apple in my hand, I acted like a child receiving a piece of candy.

"Where did you get this?" I exclaimed gleefully.

"From paradise." He smiled, pleased to see me so happy.

After a few weeks of eating good food, I felt much stronger. The **sleeping facilities** were better, too. The room we slept in was not **drafty**, as had been the case in Birkenau, and

....

sleeping facilities places where we slept
drafty cold and windy

there were fewer people to one bunk. But the greatest luxury Brünnlitz had to offer was a hot shower. It was a joy I looked forward to every week.

True to Dick's promise, I started working in the SS kitchen. My experiences serving Nazis had not been exactly pleasant, but Dick assured me I had nothing to worry about here. On my first day I was greeted with remarks I had heard before: "I hope you are clean . . . One never knows with you people . . . Soap and water, that's something dirty Jews **shy away from**, am I right?" I pretended the **slurs** were not meant for me. Instead I focused on my work, scrubbing the kitchen counters and floors until my fingers bled.

The guards who came off the night shift had to have their breakfast ready at six in the morning. After I washed their dishes and tidied the kitchen, the officers arrived for their meal. Then more cleaning and scrubbing before I started to peel potatoes and clean and chop vegetables to assist the cook. He checked my hands for cleanliness at every step, not that he washed his own.

Midway through one morning the cook **mellowed a little**. "The leftovers are kept in this corner," he said. "They are for you to eat. Just make sure you don't take any food back with you."

I had not eaten that morning. I was very hungry, and although my eyes continually glanced at the sausage and bread and leftover sweet rolls, I controlled my impulse to rush toward the food. I waited till the cook gave me permission to stop and eat.

....

shy away from do not use
slurs mean words; insults
mellowed a little was nicer to me

In spite of the fact that I still had bouts of pain in my back and abdomen, I did my job well. The kitchen sparkled. I hoped to convince the cook that his assessment of Jews had been wrong. Also, there was always the fear that he might report me to Liebholt if I did something that didn't please him.

The cook never spoke to me other than to give orders, but his insults eventually stopped and he allowed me to enter the dining room to serve food. I most feared the early mornings, when the guards came for breakfast. They were sullen men from the **provinces**. Their speech patterns and the awkwardness of their manners revealed **their humble backgrounds**. Now that they had been put into positions of power, they suddenly **felt self-important**. The fried eggs set before them, the sausages, and the sweet rolls—very little seemed to please these men. Many times I went back to the kitchen and prepared something else.

One of the guards complained almost daily. Either the rolls were too crisp or not crisp enough; the eggs, too hard or too soft. He didn't even know himself what it was he wanted, but harassing me was **a sport he seldom missed**. A heavyset man who looked to be in his forties was an especially cruel guard who beat prisoners. They nicknamed him "Crazy Johann."

One morning when he was in a bad mood, after a fight with another guard, he stormed into the kitchen. Throwing his food at me, he shouted, "Damn Jewess, the eggs are cold again. I'll report you for this to the commandant."

....

provinces countryside; small towns
their humble backgrounds that they had been poor
felt self-important acted like they were important
a sport he seldom missed something he always did

All I could think about was Commandant Liebholt possibly remembering me and sending me back to Birkenau. And that sent a chill through me.

I noticed something in Crazy Johann's speech that I'd never detected before—the **dialect he used** was from Ostfriesland, where I was born. As soon as I was able to stop shaking, I answered him in the same dialect: "I'm sorry about the eggs, sir. I will make you a better breakfast this time."

He was startled by my speech. I had never spoken to him before, only set breakfast before him.

"You speak Ostfriesisch," he said. "Where did you learn that?"

"I was born in Aurich," I answered, immediately regretting that I'd revealed that much. What if he knew my family? What if he'd had a dispute with them? I had so many uncles living in Aurich. Mama was one of twelve children.

My fears were unfounded, for he immediately became friendlier. "The Jews have long been expelled from Ostfriesland. You wouldn't find even one Jew there now." He had a big smile on his face as he told me this.

My expression **remained neutral**. *Yes,* I thought, *I know only too well what you did to us.*

"Hey, I'm from Moordorf, not far from where you lived. You know where that is?"

I knew where Moordorf was. It was one of the poorest

....

dialect he used way he spoke sounded like he
My fears were unfounded I did not need to be afraid
remained neutral did not show how I felt

villages in the area. People in Moordorf lived in mud huts. Not wanting to embarrass him, I answered, "I have been away from there for so long, I don't remember."

When he asked me if I knew a man by the name of Selly Wolff, my heart began to beat so loud that I feared he could hear the sound it was making. Should I admit that Selly Wolff had been my grandfather? He had been a successful man, something that might have **enraged Crazy Johann, given his own circumstances**. I shook my head, indicating I didn't know who Selly Wolff was. From then on Crazy Johann left me alone.

Occasionally, Herr Direktor Schindler came to the kitchen door. He always had a kind word for me. "Are they treating you right?" He made sure the SS cook heard him. "I haven't had my breakfast this morning," he continued. "Frau Schindler **neglected her wifely duties**. Will you make breakfast for me?"

I took special care to serve him the best the kitchen had to offer. But when Untersturmführer Liebholt approached, I **busied myself with** other tasks. I was still afraid of him.

The harsh winter weather finally let up, making life in Brünnlitz much easier. And the news Dick learned from listening to the radio indicated the Germans were finally losing the war.

But all was not well yet. The radio also announced the death of President Franklin Roosevelt in America. I was saddened by the news, as were all the prisoners. Our greatest hopes for

....

enraged Crazy Johann, given his own circumstances made him angry, since he was poor

neglected her wifely duties did not cook for me like wives are supposed to

busied myself with worked on

bringing Germany down had been pinned on America and its leaders. And Oskar Schindler was away from camp a good deal. Just when we got used to seeing him, he would disappear again. I knew little of the inner workings of the camp, but I was certain Schindler's disappearances had to do with our survival in Brünnlitz.

Dick was pensive and subdued these days. "Something is wrong," he said. He, too, was worried about Schindler's absences.

"Dear God!" I said out loud. "Do you think Liebholt has the power to send us back to Auschwitz?"

"Anything is possible. What concerns me is that ditches are being dug around the camp. I have a suspicion they are being prepared for us. Why send us back to Auschwitz? Liebholt can kill us here."

"Schindler will not let that happen," I said, not quite believing myself.

"You don't know the whole story. Lately Liebholt has been on the factory floor a lot. He brings inspectors with him, implying Herr Direktor Schindler is not putting out a proper product and that he is treating his Jews far too leniently. We are supposed to be **an ammunition factory making shells**. Most of the shells **are defective**—we make sure of that. Liebholt **is on to us**, and if he succeeds in his accusations, Schindler could be arrested and we will be at the mercy of this hateful man."

I stared blankly into the night. Only days earlier I had been euphoric knowing the Russians would soon be here to give us our freedom. Even the SS kitchen personnel talked about falling into Russian hands and how that would be worse than death. It was April 1945 and Oskar Schindler had still not returned. This was a time of great anxiety. Not knowing what would happen **set us all on edge**. It was the same for the SS guards. They were restless but far less demanding. Even Crazy Johann let up on his complaints. The cook talked to me for the first time about something other than the kitchen.

"Germany is not defeated yet, but if the Russians should **overrun** us, I expect you to tell them how well you were treated."

"Of course," I answered, thinking, ***Don't count on that.*** Besides, I didn't know that I was safe either. Liebholt might kill me first.

Then one day Oskar Schindler returned. On April 28 he celebrated his thirty-seventh birthday. That night I met Dick at the wire fence that divided the men's quarters from the women's. Dick seemed a little drunk. I knew the signs. From time to time the underground smuggled in vodka, and Dick had a liking for it. On those nights he swayed a little, as he did now.

"Schindler made a speech in honor of his birthday. He was drunk."

"What did he say?"

"He was daring in his contempt for the Nazis, saying the

....

set us all on edge made all of us nervous
overrun capture, defeat
Don't count on that. *I will never tell them that.*

Third Reich was soon coming to an end. He even addressed the SS men who were present, letting them know they were now the prisoners behind Brünnlitz's walls."

"This speech could get him—and all of us—into trouble. What if Liebholt hears about it?"

Dick agreed and then went back to listen to the radio. I was already asleep when Hella returned from the fence to tell me the latest.

"Wake up! This is important. Liebholt has left Brünnlitz. He is on his way to the Russian front. It was Oskar Schindler's doing."

This was unbelievable news!

★ ★ ★

A little over a week later Oskar Schindler assembled all of us. He announced: "What I have to say is important. I want you to listen carefully. Germany has **unconditionally** surrendered. I have just listened to the **BBC** and to Churchill's victory speech. We have been through a lot together, but what we hoped for has finally happened."

Except for Dick and his comrades, who already knew of the surrender, we were stunned at the words we had longed to hear for such a long time. Schindler paused only briefly.

"I have one more thing to ask of you. Do not **take the law into your own hands**. It's not up to you to take revenge. The

....

unconditionally absolutely

BBC British Broadcasting Company; news on a British radio station

take the law into your own hands act out against the Nazis

murderers will have to be judged in a court of law."

As Schindler talked the SS guards quietly left the hall. Only we prisoners remained, **mesmerized by** what we heard.

It was impossible to absorb the meaning of freedom. But it was over. The nightmare had come to an end.

★ ★ ★

I had a dreadful dream that wouldn't leave me, even though I was fully awake now. "We are free, we are free," people kept shouting, only I was being dragged into a furnace that resembled the crematorium in Birkenau.

Struggling to pull myself from the nightmare, I walked down the stairs of my barrack to get out into the open. People were talking freely with one another. "It's May 8th, 1945," someone called out. The date **triggered a memory**. It was Mama's birthday today, exactly three years since we were deported from Weimar. The lilac tree would be in bloom, but Papa would never sing the birthday song again. And only God knew whether Mama and Wolfgang were still alive.

Eva came looking for me. "Where have you been?" she wanted to know. "Come, upstairs **there is a feast going on**."

Dick stood at the entrance to the camp, a gun slung over his shoulder. He was not happy to see Eva and me.

"It's not safe to walk around," he said. "Some Germans are still **holding out** around here. Go back inside. Both of you."

....

mesmerized by unable to move because of
triggered a memory made me remember something
there is a feast going on where people are eating
holding out fighting and shooting people

"But it's over, didn't Schindler say so? The Germans surrendered," I said.

"Officially it's over, but there is still some shooting going on. Do as I tell you. I'll come to see you later. And make sure to keep Eva with you."

Once inside Eva and I were greeted with giddy excitement. Spread out on the floor was a blanket covered with delicacies: cheese, salami, sausage, and lots of bread. We were invited to join the feast.

"Where did all this food come from?" I asked.

"We went into the village," Hella's older brother said. "It's the very least they could do for us. The good **burghers of** Brünnlitz thought we contaminated the air here. They petitioned Berlin to send us back to Auschwitz or some other horrible place."

Toward evening Dick arrived with more food, including hot water and a tin of tea. "You once told me how much you loved tea." He handed me the treasures, but then he was eager to get away.

I pleaded with him to stay, but his mind was **elsewhere**. The camp was not safe from German **reprisal**. He was needed to guard the entrance.

Two days later Dick came running up the stairs of the women's quarters. He was in high spirits. His eyes shone, his

---

burghers of people who lived in
elsewhere thinking about something else
reprisal punishment, revenge

cheeks were flushed; I had never seen him look so strong, so vital.

"Come with me," he shouted as he reached for my hand. His own was clammy with excitement. "We don't want to miss the Russians' arrival. They are at the gate now!"

Caught up in the exhilaration of the moment, I ran with him to the camp's square, where a slightly built Russian officer on horseback was **dismounting**. He had come alone and was immediately surrounded. Dick stepped forward, still holding my hand, pulling me with him.

"Welcome, our liberator!" he shouted in Russian.

We started to cry and laugh at the same time. The Russian did nothing to stop our hysteria. Instead tears welled up in his eyes as he spoke. Dick translated the Russians words. "I am a Hebrew, like you. And so, my **brethren, it is fitting** that I give you your freedom. You can walk out of here at any time. We are making plans to **expedite it**."

A great silence met the Russian's unbelievable words, soon followed by jubilant cries in many languages and dialects, all carrying the same message:

We are free! We are free!

★ ★ ★

....

dismounting getting off his horse
brethren, it is fitting brothers and sisters, it is only right
expedite it help you leave here quickly

Dick and Hannelore Hillman with the Jewish army chaplain (center), who married them in Erding, Bavaria.

Hannelore Wolff and Bernard (Dick) Hillman were married on October 22, 1945. They arrived in New York on January 4, 1947.

Except for two sisters, neither Hannelore nor Dick ever heard from their loved ones again.

BEFORE YOU MOVE ON...

1. **Inference** Reread page 194. Why did Schindler direct his workers to make defective ammunition?

2. **Comparisons** Reread pages 198–199. How did the mood change when the Russians arrived?